CAMBRIDGE LIBRARY COLLECTION

Books of enduring scholarly value

Cambridge

The city of Cambridge received its royal charter in 1201, having already been home to Britons, Romans and Anglo-Saxons for many centuries. Cambridge University was founded soon afterwards and celebrates its octocentenary in 2009. This series explores the history and influence of Cambridge as a centre of science, learning, and discovery, its contributions to national and global politics and culture, and its inevitable controversies and scandals.

Architecture in Cambridge

First published in 1942, Theodore Fyfe's book on Cambridge architecture was written to 'enable the visitor to Cambridge to realise the value of the Town and University for illustrating the sequence of styles in English architecture'. Including over fifty drawings of both famous and lesser-known Cambridge architectural sights, and a glossary giving clear definitions of technical architectural terms, the book remains a valuable guide for the modern visitor. The Introduction outlines the principal English architectural styles, from Romanesque to Gothic to Renaissance, the periods during which they flourished, and their significant characteristics. Fyfe then analyses over thirty selected Cambridge examples in detail, including a description of the Perpendicular Gothic style as exemplified on a grand scale by the world-famous King's College Chapel – 'the glory of Cambridge'.

Cambridge University Press has long been a pioneer in the reissuing of out-of-print titles from its own backlist, producing digital reprints of books that are still sought after by scholars and students but could not be reprinted economically using traditional technology. The Cambridge Library Collection extends this activity to a wider range of books which are still of importance to researchers and professionals, either for the source material they contain, or as landmarks in the history of their academic discipline.

Drawing from the world-renowned collections in the Cambridge University Library, and guided by the advice of experts in each subject area, Cambridge University Press is using state-of-the-art scanning machines in its own Printing House to capture the content of each book selected for inclusion. The files are processed to give a consistently clear, crisp image, and the books finished to the high quality standard for which the Press is recognised around the world. The latest print-on-demand technology ensures that the books will remain available indefinitely, and that orders for single or multiple copies can quickly be supplied.

The Cambridge Library Collection will bring back to life books of enduring scholarly value across a wide range of disciplines in the humanities and social sciences and in science and technology.

Architecture in Cambridge

Examples of Architectural Styles from Saxon to Modern Times

DAVID THEODORE FYFE

CAMBRIDGE
UNIVERSITY PRESS

CAMBRIDGE UNIVERSITY PRESS

Cambridge New York Melbourne Madrid Cape Town Singapore São Paolo Delhi

Published in the United States of America by Cambridge University Press, New York

www.cambridge.org
Information on this title: www.cambridge.org/9781108002417

© in this compilation Cambridge University Press 2009

This edition first published 1942
This digitally printed version 2009

ISBN 978-1-108-00241-7

The 'Gate of Virtue', Gonville and Caius College; west side

Architecture in Cambridge

Examples of English architectural styles from Saxon to Modern times

by

THEODORE FYFE

M.A., F.R.I.B.A.

*Sometime Lecturer in Architecture and
Director of the School of Architecture
in the University of Cambridge*

with an Introduction and fifty-four illustrations

CAMBRIDGE

AT THE UNIVERSITY PRESS

1942

CAMBRIDGE
UNIVERSITY PRESS
LONDON: BENTLEY HOUSE

NEW YORK, TORONTO, BOMBAY
CALCUTTA, MADRAS: MACMILLAN

PRINTED IN GREAT BRITAIN

To the Memory of

PROFESSOR SIR ALBERT C. SEWARD

CONTENTS

INTRODUCTION and NOTES

vii

PLATES AND DESCRIPTIONS

GLOSSARY

INDEX

x

FIGURES IN THE TEXT

xi

PREFACE

This book may enable the architecturally-minded visitor to Cambridge—who has more leisure than can be afforded in a brief inspection—to realise the value of the Town and University for illustrating the sequence of styles in English architecture; for which purpose, the series of thirty-one Plates and Descriptions of subjects from Cambridge has been augmented by an Introduction dealing with England as a whole. In this, again, subjects from Cambridge have been used for the most part, though no excuse should be required for the frequent reference to Ely Cathedral; and only by its inclusion with Cambridge can Gothic architecture, as a whole, be adequately explained.

The examples have been selected as typical of the more important aspects of architectural *style*, without consideration of the inclusion of all the Colleges; the only explanation that need be offered for the omission of Magdalene and Sidney Sussex. A more solid objection might be maintained to the omission of one of the timber-framed domestic buildings in the Town; but these buildings show rather a phase of construction than of style, belonging to a type which was widely prevalent and unvarying in essentials.

There have been so many books on Cambridge that I may, perhaps, be excused for not mentioning any of them except Willis and Clark's great work, and the late J. W. Clark's *A Concise Guide to the Town and University of Cambridge*, now in its eleventh edition; to these, and to the former in particular, I have been much indebted. The present work was begun many years ago and has been laid aside more than once, but it has been a labour of love and the illustrations, with their many deficiencies, were all drawn on the spot by myself. I have inscribed it to the Memory of the late Sir Albert Seward, who, when he was Master of Downing, was actually responsible for its inception and general form. Shortly before his death, he accepted its dedication to himself. In the early stages of production, without his enthusiasm for its main purpose, the book might never have been realised.

I wish to thank Mr Hugh Easton for encouragement and advice about the illustrations; Dr Ellis Minns for information about Pembroke College; Mr W. Parker Dyson for reading through the Introduction; and my son-in-law, Captain Michael Gillilan, for reading through the Descriptions of the Plates. In addition, I wish to express my deep indebtedness to the Staff of the Cambridge University Press; particularly to Mr W. Lewis, the University Printer.

THEODORE FYFE

Longstowe Hall, Cambridgeshire
January, 1942

INTRODUCTION
and
NOTES

INTRODUCTION

Cambridge can show to a remarkable extent the continuity of the architecture of England from later Saxon times to the present day. We could never expect the buildings of a single town to be quite comprehensive, but possibly no other English centre is so completely equipped: Oxford, which is more representative in some respects, notably for Norman work, has no outstanding example of either Saxon or Early Gothic; and Cambridge is also more representative because Oxford has stone buildings only; but brick was an important building material in England from the beginning of the sixteenth century onwards, and in some centres—Cambridge being one of them—it was in use from the later part of the fifteenth century. The very limitations of its constructive and decorative possibilities gave the brick building a value of its own.

STYLES IN ENGLISH ARCHITECTURE

There is no more common form of question put to the historian of architecture than 'How are we to know that a building belongs to a particular style or period?' We must begin with *construction*, as in any consideration of architectural styles we cannot ignore the limitations of particular materials; and what we call a 'style' was something which was made by a gradual process, controlled, more or less strictly, by local methods of handling materials. The vertical projecting strips, for example, that we often find in Saxon towers, may have had a remote origin far removed from England, but the constructive method of building these strips in Saxon walls is peculiarly native; and we could find similar explanations for many distinctive forms in other countries. In such ways arose much of the expression of architecture as we know it. In England, as in other countries, its various phases have been classified in terms that will be used here in considering English 'styles', or in greater detail, 'periods'.

All these local groupings, however, are governed by the large phases of expression that were common to Europe in general. Thus, in England, the Saxon and Norman buildings erected before the end of the twelfth century were versions of the ROMANESQUE style; and from that time till the middle of the sixteenth century, buildings show versions of the GOTHIC or POINTED style: more broadly still, all of this, from Saxon to the beginnings of Renaissance, can be classified as MEDIAEVAL.

Before any further definitions of particular styles or periods are attempted, the practical fact that a building rises from its *plan* should not be overlooked; and because the plan is the form of a building as laid out on the ground, it is bound to influence the form of the upper structure. Thus, the prevailing form of the large Early Christian church, one of the most important types of Mediaeval building left to us, was based on a particular kind of Roman building known as the 'basilica'; and the motive for the adoption of this form was a practical one, arising from a type of plan that made the construction of roofs simple; while it gave also ample light, ample space and full processional facilities.

Broadly speaking, all building expression in England during the 1100 years that elapsed from the end of the seventh till the end of the eighteenth centuries is classifiable into the three stylistic terms of ROMANESQUE, GOTHIC and RENAISSANCE; of which some more precise definition should now be given.

We call buildings 'Romanesque'—in this country, Saxon
and Norman buildings—in the first place, because, where the
arch was used for arcades or for openings such as doors and
windows, it had the round (i.e. semicircular) form, and this
form was a Roman one; in the second place, because, as
mentioned already, the larger Early Christian churches
adopted an established Roman type of structure; this latter
reason being important, because a building may be Romanesque without having arches, and the earliest Christian
basilicas in Rome used the lintel, the original Classical
medium for spanning all openings. Lastly, there was a
direct though more accidental connection between Roman
buildings and the earlier Christian churches, because many
of these churches used, for their internal (and occasionally
external) supports, the valuable marble or porphyry columns
of disused Roman temples or secular buildings.

When all is said, however, the use of the *round arch* is the
most easily understood sign that a Mediaeval building is
Romanesque. The Saxon Romanesque arch was usually built
in one ring of stones or bricks, unornamented, like the
Roman arch; but the more important arches in Norman
Romanesque were built in receding planes of two or more
rings, often carved with ornament★ (see Plates II and III and
Fig. 1*a*).

Saxon buildings were never—so far as we know—of great
size, and the walling of those left to us is comparatively thin,
though better constructed than it appears to be. In Norman
masonry we find small *short* squared stones that were used
as a facing to a poorer form of construction in the core of the
wall, especially in the larger buildings, where walls and

★ Each individual stone on the face of an arch-ring is still called in England
by the French term *voussoir*.

pillars were usually much more massive than would have been necessary if the construction had been better; but though we may be willing to admit that space was thereby wasted, our appreciation of architecture is fortunately not dependent on a sense of its mechanical efficiency, and we

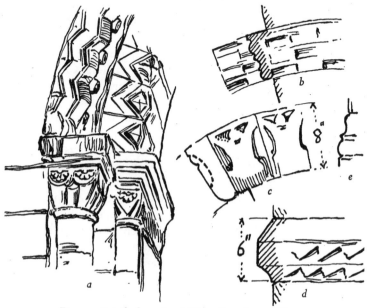

Fig. 1. Details from Sturbridge Chapel, twelfth century.
a—chancel arch. *b* and *c*—external arch-rings. *d*—external wall-band.
e—external shaft-base.

cannot withhold our admiration for the amplitude and grandeur of Norman architecture, with its amazing contrast to the constructive ability of the succeeding period in the middle of the thirteenth century, when vaulting was assembled on a single clustered shaft of Purbeck marble, so slight that it is hard to believe it is not made of iron.

GOTHIC

The 'Early English' period of Gothic developed without any sense of effort from Norman Romanesque, the successor of the Saxon Romanesque that prevailed in England from the end of the seventh century till the Norman Conquest, or even later. The beginnings of Gothic can be seen to great advantage at Ely Cathedral, in the late twelfth century work of the upper part of the south-western tower; where the window arches, though pointed, have a blunt form hardly distinguishable from a semicircle. This form, used with the receding planes that were characteristic of Norman arches, is called 'Transitional', i.e. a bridge between Norman and Early English, and the term is appropriate as marking the beginning of the far-reaching developments of *pointed arch* construction; but it should be noted that Transitional arches were often round, and when pointed, were not always blunt. The chancel arch of that period in Soham Church, near Cambridge, for example, has a normal pointed form; while it should also be noted that many arches of the Early English period were blunt, and that this characteristic was often intensified by the great mass of deeply undercut mouldings surmounted by the hood-mould,★ composing the arch (see Fig. 2).

L–*Label*. LS–*Label stop*. S–*Purbeck Shaft*
P¹–*Penetration of window head and splayed jamb*
P²–*Penetration of arched soffite with jamb and head.*

Fig. 2. The 'Abbey Church' (St Andrew the Less). First half of thirteenth century.

★ Sometimes called a 'label', or 'label-mould'.

Side by side with this kind of arch we get the more sharply-pointed Early English form that can be seen, for example, in Westminster Abbey.

Gothic architecture is the style of the pointed arch and the pointed vault; in England, passing through three well-defined phases or periods, that it has been found convenient to name 'Early English', 'Decorated', and 'Perpendicular'; these terms being broadly synonymous with the thirteenth, fourteenth and fifteenth centuries.*

Questions that will arise naturally are

(1) *How are we to distinguish these three phases of Gothic architecture in England?*

(2) *When did the Gothic style of building end?*

Some information about both of these questions will be found in the descriptions of Pls. IV to XVII: it can be supplemented as follows:

THE DISTINGUISHING CHARACTERISTICS OF THE GOTHIC PHASES IN ENGLAND

It is best to begin with *window* treatments. In EARLY ENGLISH Gothic we find single undivided windows, sometimes of considerable height, but narrow in proportion (Pl. IV); windows of this type being known as 'lancets', sometimes grouped in twos or threes without any loss to their individual character; a treatment that is also found in late Norman work, used with round arches.

* Just as Norman is broadly synonymous with the twelfth century. The periods, stated more exactly (J. H. Parker's classification has been followed), were: Norman 1100–1175; Transitional 1175–1200; Early English 1200–1275; Decorated (Early) 1275–1325, (Late) 1325–1375; Perpendicular (Early) 1375–1425, (Late) 1425–1525. It will be seen that at least 75 per cent of each particular period, taken as a whole, falls into one century.

The next development in windows—again based on Norman precedent—was the closer grouping of two or three lancets, with a plain geometrical opening or openings above the group, the whole of these enclosed in a single outer arch; the result being known as 'plate tracery', associated with the first half of the thirteenth century, of which an example—difficult to see—can be found in the upper storey of the tower in Jesus College Chapel.

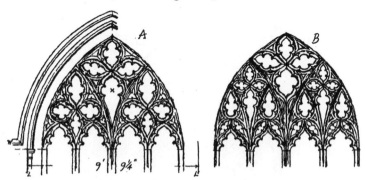

Fig. 3. St Mary the Less, fourteenth century.
A—Third window, north.   B—Fourth window, north.

The next step was the grouping of these assembled units in two or groups of two 'lights' surmounted by moulded and cusped[1] tracery, using circular forms and enclosed in moulded outer arches, the division bars of the lights being more elaborate. This result is called 'geometrical tracery'; it is associated with the summit of English Gothic in the last two quarters of the thirteenth century, seen at its best in the great Cistercian Abbeys, notably Tintern.

The next step was the DECORATED period of the fourteenth century, when windows were often of larger area and were composed of many lights divided by thin mullions (or upright stone division-bars), surmounted by elaborate tracery that gradually developed freedom of line; this later phase of 'flowing tracery' belongs to the second and third quarters of the fourteenth century (see Pl. V and Fig. 3 for examples that border on 'geometrical').

Lastly, we get the PERPENDICULAR phase, introduced at the end of the fourteenth century, when the controlling lines of all the tracery were upright (Fig. 4). At first, the

Little St. Mary's

Fig. 4. A.D. 1447.

window-arches that enclosed the tracery were of normal pointed form, but as the phase progressed, they were raised at the springing, giving increased light and becoming more flattened though still pointed; and as each side had to be set out from two curves instead of one, the result was what is known as the 'four-centred' arch (see Figs. 5, 6 and 7). A more unusual form, occasionally used in the fifteenth century, where each side of the arch is a simple though flat curve, can be seen at Cambridge in the aisles of St

Botolph's Church (Pl. VII) and the west window of St Michael's Church in Trinity Street. Perpendicular windows introduced another element—the stiffening of mullions by arched *transoms*★ (see Fig. 4, and Fig. 8 for a later example) —that had an important influence on future development.

Though window treatment is one of the surest guides, there are other distinguishing marks of the various phases of Mediaeval building in England: many of them will be referred to in the descriptions of the Plates. The most conspicuous are to be found in the character and decoration of what are termed in architecture 'mouldings', which may be defined as the linear elaboration, out of the squared form, of any clearly marked and continuous members of a building. Early Gothic is the most practical and forthright style in existence, and the clever development of its moulded

Fig. 5. Queens' College, c. 1460.

forms shows an inevitable process that is both logical and fascinating. The primary squared forms from which the rings of moulded and decorated Norman arches were cut can be seen clearly in Pl. II, while we can see the same logical process in the Early English mouldings shown in Fig. 2 and Pl. IV, both examples exhibiting the contrast of richly moulded arches with the deep plain window-reveals that were a feature of thirteenth century work; but it should be noted that the arch-mouldings were carried on the capitals

★ A transom is the horizontal cross-bar of a mullioned window.

of round pillars called 'shafts', that ran down to the sill-table and sometimes even to the floor. These shafts, which were usually quite detached (see Fig. 9), are an outstanding characteristic of Early English Gothic; though, again, we find their beginnings in Norman work—see Pls. II and III.

Towards the very end of the thirteenth century, and during the fourteenth, mouldings tended to be less con-

Great St. Mary's

Fig. 6. Late fifteenth century.

structive,* as they were produced from stones that were larger than those of the squared forms in receding planes that are characteristic of Norman and Early English work; and this tendency was accentuated in the Perpendicular work of the fifteenth century.

Our knowledge of Gothic architecture is gained mostly from ecclesiastical buildings, in which masonry could be

* At first, arch-mouldings were elaborate, but on more even planes than in Early English; admirably shown in Mr T. D. Atkinson's *Glossary*, Fig. 152.

exploited to a remarkable extent; for Gothic was pre-eminently an architecture of small stone construction, and a great deal of its expression was due to the handling of practical features—the string-course, the corbel table and the buttress weathering, for rain protection; the buttress for thrust resistance; the rib as the chief element in vault structure—and we are apt to forget that these, like most architectural forms, were utilitarian in origin.[2]

Fig. 7. Early sixteenth century.   Fig. 8.

TUDOR ARCHITECTURE AND THE INTRO-
DUCTION OF RENAISSANCE

The steps that produced TUDOR architecture—the last phase of Mediaeval architecture in England—culminating in the reign of Queen Elizabeth—are again bound up with window treatments, as the arched transom and the arched head in mullioned windows were found to be less convenient for domestic work than their simple translation into square form. In Fig. 6 we can see a usual form of late Perpendicular door-head, and although it is arched, it has a

13

squared label;* while in Fig. 14 we can see a domestic example of a window—a little later in date—where the use of the squared label is the only admissible one.

The progressive steps can be seen perfectly in Jesus College Gateway (Pl. XI) and in Great Gate, Trinity (Pl. XIII); the simplified *Elizabethan* window, that finally dispensed with the arch and made possible the consistent use of rectangular leaded-glass panes, instead of diamond-shaped panes, being a perfectly logical process of the first importance, because it prepared the way for the lintelled window heads that were a fundamental principle in the Classical style re-discovered by the architects of the Renaissance. In a word, towards the end of the sixteenth century in England, the way was already prepared for the *rectilinear* (or *Classical*) principle in architecture, as opposed to the *curvilinear* principle that was inseparable from *Mediaeval* construction; the transom, introduced for strength in the Perpendicular period, being a leading factor in the whole process.

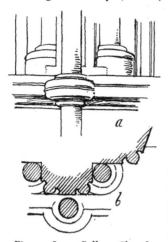

Fig. 9. Jesus College Chapel, thirteenth century. *a*—Shafting at sill-table, north side. *b*—The same in plan.

The domestic development of late Tudor architecture is of the utmost importance. It adhered to the large amount of window area that characterised the greater Perpendicular churches, and the deep bays of the halls of large houses of

* This form produced the spandrel, ornamented with geometrical patterns (as in Fig. 6) or heraldic shields, or conventionalised foliage.

the period, somewhat similar to the slightly later ones in the Hall of Trinity College, Cambridge; the control of window subdivisions, by the fixed sizes of the small rectangular leaded panes already mentioned, being consistent with present-day practice in the use of standardised metal windows.

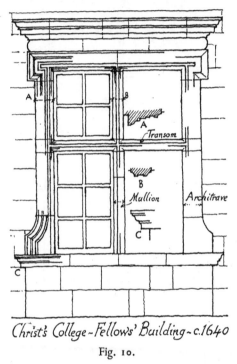

Christ's College - Fellows' Building - c.1640

Fig. 10.

This phase of English architecture, that can be seen at Audley End and other large mansions of the period, dominated the last half of the sixteenth century and the beginning of the seventeenth: after this time Classical details—at first timidly introduced—tended to make buildings more Renaissance than Mediaeval. The 'Brick Building' of

Emmanuel College, however, built in 1633, is more Mediaeval than Renaissance; while the Fellows' Building at

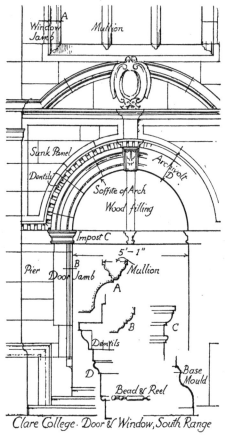

Clare College. Door & Window, South Range

Fig. 11.

Christ's College, built in 1640, is distinctly more Renaissance than Mediaeval, though there are Mediaeval features in it, and it is interesting to compare its treatment—the windows in particular—with that of the exactly contemporary south range of Clare College (Figs. 10 and 11). By this time we have passed from the *Elizabethan* or late Tudor phase, and the *Jacobean* phase that followed it with hardly a perceptible change, into the middle STUART period, which it is sometimes convenient to term *Carolean*.

We can be reasonably certain that any building that is Jacobean, i.e. erected in the reign of James I (1603–1625), will have Classical details; but here and there we find buildings such as the Hall at Trinity College (1604), the south range of the second ('Ivy') Court at Pembroke College (Pl. XVI), or Peterhouse Chapel (Pl. XIV), erected during or even after this reign, that were admittedly backward, as their Mediaeval elements are so strongly marked. The famous Gates erected by Dr Caius at Gonville and Caius College— the 'Gate of Virtue' (1567) and the unique little monument called the 'Gate of Honour' (c. 1569)—are significant as showing that quite early Elizabethan work could be Classical, even in form.★ It is difficult, therefore, from observation, to tell the exact date of any building erected in the latter part of the sixteenth century or the first half of the seventeenth.

The late Stuart phase, closing with the reigns of *William and Mary*, and of *Queen Anne*, saw the introduction of what is termed 'Full Renaissance', not really consolidated before Sir Christopher Wren had built Pembroke College Chapel, Cambridge, in 1663–64; after which date, till the end of the GEORGIAN period, we get variations on one particular theme, that of fully-established Renaissance; although, as will be pointed out farther on, Mediaeval forms never wholly died out.

We can therefore summarise these remarks by saying that, roughly speaking, from the accession of Elizabeth in 1558 till the end of the reign of James I in 1625, architecture was

★ See Frontispiece; also, below, pp. 30 n. and 32.

slowly adapting itself from Mediaeval to Renaissance; that in this time and till 1663 (shortly after the Restoration) we get *Immature Renaissance*; and that from 1663 onwards we get *Full and Later Renaissance*.

In comparison with the simplicity of the Gothic subdivisions, those of Tudor and Renaissance may seem confusing, but the terms 'Tudor', 'Stuart' and 'Georgian' have been stressed because they are approximately representative of the sixteenth, seventeenth and eighteenth centuries; 'Renaissance', in some form or another, being visible throughout except in the earlier Tudor period. Of the minor terms, 'Elizabethan' and 'Jacobean' are the most in general use.

DUTCH AND FLEMISH INFLUENCES

The form of the gables of Peterhouse Chapel (see Pl. XIV) shows an example of an influence that came from Holland and Belgium in the seventeenth century, resulting in various shapings of the straight-sided gables that had been used consistently in English domestic architecture; though these were often decorated with 'finials', as shown in Pl. XVI and in greater detail in Fig. 12. Examples in Cambridge of shaped or 'Dutch' gables can be seen at St John's College (south-west corner of third court where it abuts on the river, and dated

Fig. 12. Pembroke College, 1661.

1671)—Fig. 13, at Emmanuel College (south end of the Brick Building, 1633–34) and at Trinity Hall—Fig. 14; this last showing an earlier stepped form that is probably contemporary with the rest of the building to which it belongs.

The shaped gables date usually from the second or third quarters of the seventeenth century, being met with where

St. John's
1671

Fig. 13.

Trinity Hall

Fig. 14. Mid-sixteenth century.

brickwork prevailed—particularly in the eastern counties—
as they are peculiarly associated with that material; often
wholly executed in it, though the copings are sometimes of
stone.*

RENAISSANCE

An endeavour has been made to explain the terms Romanesque and Gothic, to outline the main phases of each of these
styles, and to indicate that if there was not exactly a natural
evolution—through Tudor architecture—from Gothic to
Renaissance, there was no abrupt break. Lastly, the phases
of Renaissance in England—Immature, Full and Later—have
been mentioned, and the term 'Classical' has been introduced as synonymous with 'Renaissance'; but it is advisable
that the meaning of 'Renaissance' as applied to architecture
in general should be explained further.

There were two main tendencies in the architecture
broadly called Classical—i.e. architecture in Eastern Europe
and the Near East from the sixth century B.C. till the fourth
century A.D.—one of which perfected or continued forms
that had evolved naturally from early Greek buildings,
while the other was merely a matter of the *treatment* of
vaulted and domical buildings depending on the Roman
use of concrete.

The first of these tendencies produced the Early Christian
basilican churches of the fourth to the seventh centuries
(see above, p. 5), that were simply constructed and had
wooden roofs; but nearly coincident in date with this development—seen at its best in Rome—was another one in

* For an excellent survey of the subject, well illustrated, see C. L.
Cudworth, 'The Dutch Gables of East Anglia', in *The Architectural Review*,
March 1939.

Greece and the Near East, known as the 'Byzantine', that was undoubtedly influenced both by advanced Roman structures and by Oriental sources, resulting in an architecture of brick, characterised by domical vaults and domes of a more daring nature than the Romans ever achieved. The Byzantine style had practically no influence on the architecture of the West, though it was absorbed by the Ottoman Turks; but, on the other hand, the second tendency—that of Roman treatments—produced. Renaissance architecture, one aspect of the renewal of Classical culture in all its forms, early in the fifteenth century, that affected Western Europe so profoundly: architecture—more or less quickly—became a matter of resurrecting the Classical treatments that Brunelleschi, the San Galli and others had found ready to hand in the ruins of Rome. Wren was proud to consider his work as being in the 'Roman manner'.

IMPORTANCE OF CIVIL AND DOMESTIC BUILDINGS

Ecclesiastical buildings adhered to Mediaeval forms more tenaciously than civil buildings (Peterhouse Chapel has already been mentioned), and it was domestic convenience, as we have seen, that produced the squared form of the semi-Mediaeval Elizabethan window; though, before this, Italian architects had evolved full Renaissance, and their civil and larger domestic buildings had become variants of the mature treatments of later Classical times. In 1621—i.e. before the second court of Pembroke College was built— Inigo Jones, as a direct result of study in Italy, had given us this full Renaissance type of building, quite exceptional in this country, in the Banqueting House that still survives in Whitehall as the only fragment of the great palace that he designed for the Sovereign.

What do we find in this type of building? We find
(1) the division of the wall surface into the component
parts of approved Classical usage, i.e. the *base*, the *main
wall-field*, the *entablature*,* and the *attic*;
(2) window and door openings—usually, though not in-
variably, as single units—embellished with a Classical as
opposed to a Mediaeval treatment;
(3) the possible use of an Order or Orders.

ORDERS

An 'Order' may be defined as the essential post and beam
element in Classical architecture—i.e. the column and its
entablature—stylised as 'Doric', 'Ionic', 'Corinthian', or
'Composite'. An Order, however, must stand on something, and that of a Greek temple stood on a slightly raised
platform (or 'stylobate') graded into steps; differing only in
degree from the way that the Order of the Senate House at
Cambridge stands on its low base. We get thus two main
horizontal elements in a Classical building—the *base*, and the
entablature or essential beam element of the whole treatment; and it is most important to note that *these horizontal
elements are inseparable from any building that can be called
Classical or Renaissance, whether or not it has an Order treatment,*
i.e. whether or not it has the vertical element introduced
by columns or pilasters; as can be seen excellently at
Downing College, designed by William Wilkins in 1806,
where there are no Orders on the east and west ranges,
except at their ends (Fig. 21).

* If not a full entablature, at any rate a cornice (see Pls. XX, XXV and
XXVII).

The term 'curvilinear' has been used to define a main
characteristic of Gothic architecture, because Gothic was
primarily the style of the curved vault that was produced
by the pointed arch; but if *Gothic* is *curvilinear*, it is also
vertical, and reference to the outside of King's College
Chapel will show the vertical element pronouncedly, while
reference to the inside of the Chapel will show both curvilinear and vertical elements. In contradistinction, *Renaissance* architecture is *rectilinear and horizontal*. If we compare
King's College Chapel with the Senate House (see Pls. VIII
and XXVI) we can see that the Chapel is most obviously a
building of vertical character, while the Senate House, on
the other hand—a Full Renaissance building with a vertical
element in its pilastered Order—is markedly horizontal because of the preponderance of its continuous entablature and
base; and is also quite obviously rectilinear.

It cannot be emphasised too strongly that the essential
component elements in a Renaissance treatment—the base,
the main wall-field and the entablature with (usually) an
attic—and the use of classical detail throughout, are present
in any building of this style; and that it is immaterial if there
are two or three storeys, or if the definition of these storeys
is marked by subsidiary horizontal elements with or without
Orders; or if there are round-arched openings.* Occasionally, as at Emmanuel College (Pl. XXIV), we see a
mastering Order through three storeys, a principle that
can also be seen as a two-storeyed application in Wren's
Chapel at the same College (Pl. XVIII).[3]

There are, of course, buildings where neither the vertical

---

* The round (i.e. semicircular) form was always used for *arched* openings
in Renaissance architecture.

nor the horizontal elements are strongly pronounced, and England has many charming examples of this kind; three in Cambridge being shown in Plates XV, XVI and XXIV. The maintenance of a proper balance between vertical and horizontal elements in the designing of buildings is one of the main preoccupations of the modern architect.

CARVING, ORNAMENT AND DECORATION

Few things are more indicative of the outlook of a particular age than the character of its architectural ornament. The embellishment of architecture by means of sculpture and carving should consist in the emphasis of certain features in the manner of its time, produced (as it always was in greater or less degree during the historic periods) by the delight of the more skilled craftsmen in the finer aspects of their work. Certain stylistic conventions were, however, observed in each period, particularly in Renaissance times; even then, though ornament was based to a large extent on 'pattern book' types, the power to produce individual work was present everywhere, though there were, no doubt, localised schools of carvers who were in demand for exceptionally important works. As we are concerned with England alone, we may merely note here that the quality of English sculpture and carving, throughout the periods we have considered, was generally of a high order, and that at certain times it was outstanding in comparison with any contemporary European work.

There are, broadly speaking, two kinds of architectural carvings:

(1) the emphasis of certain surfaces, usually moulded, by formal patterns or repeating motives;

(2) the treatment of particular features or surfaces with free carving or with sculpture.

Saxon Romanesque. Beyond what is said in the description to Pl. I, nothing need be added here about Saxon sculpture and carving; except to remark that the small amount of work of the kind in stone that is left to us, shows that at the end of the seventh century, such productions, by the Northumbrian School, were unequalled in Europe.

The *Norman Romanesque* of the later eleventh and the twelfth centuries was conspicuous for its carved formal pattern decoration: at Cambridge, Sturbridge Chapel (Pls. II and III and Fig. 1) shows this quite clearly, and in larger and more important works, such as Durham Cathedral, the whole of a round supporting pillar might be decorated with a zig-zag or other carved pattern; due to foreign influence, as the Normans imitated marble veining and decorative forms of Near Eastern origin. When, as in the prior's door at Ely Cathedral (such examples are comparatively rare), we find a rich treatment, that included sculpture, of the whole of an important feature, we can look for the main sources in Anglo-Saxon England.

Early English Gothic can show some sculpture of a particularly high order, and it is not too much to say that no building style in the world has produced finer work of this kind than that of some schools of carving in England in the middle of the thirteenth century; work that is almost comparable with that of Greece in the fifth century B.C. and even more spontaneous, i.e., more the natural flowering of stonework just where it is needed. The angels in the spandrels of the triforium in the south transept of Westminster Abbey★ show such work at its very best, and some of the work at Lincoln Cathedral is in the same class.

★ Figs. 1 and 283 in Prior and Gardner's *Mediaeval Figure Sculpture in England* (Cambridge, 1912).

There was some formal carving also in English thirteenth-century Gothic—diaper patterning of surfaces, and the use of the 'dog-tooth' carried on from late twelfth century Transitional—but the finest work that is purely archi-tectural can be seen in the capitals and vault bosses of the more important ecclesiastical or monastic buildings, which, at their best, show a conventionalised treatment of foliage that has never been surpassed. It is fortunate that Cambridge possesses, in the cloister of Jesus College Chapel, some minor and fairly adequate ex-amples (see Fig. 15); but much more accomplished workmanship can be seen in Bishop Northwold's Presbytery (Retro-Choir) at Ely Cathedral, in the carved capitals of the pier arches and triforium, the exquisite relief carving of conventional foliage on the wall surfaces of the triforium, and some superb vault bosses.* This work dates from about 1235 and is all (except the bosses) of Purbeck marble.

Fig. 15. Jesus College, thirteenth century.

In *fourteenth-century Gothic* ('Decorated') the carving of capitals with foliage was continued, but in a more natural-istic way; of this the supreme examples can be seen in Southwell Minster; but the fourteenth century carried the embellishment of other structural features by sculpture—for such it really was—further than the thirteenth century: vaulting had become more complicated, offering oppor-tunities in the intersections of the lierne ribs in addition to the large bosses at the main rib intersections, and superb works of this kind can be seen in many English Cathedrals: as being comparatively near Cambridge and easily observed,

* For the bosses, see T. D. Atkinson's *Monastic Buildings of Ely*, Pl. XIII (Cambridge, 1933).

those in the Cloisters at Norwich may be mentioned.* Other carved work in which the fourteenth century excelled were in the ends of hood-moulds (see Figs. 16 and 17),† and of

Fig. 16. Wall tomb: manner of the fourteenth century.

corbelled vaulting shafts, and the corbels carrying roof trusses; examples of all of these can be seen in many parish churches throughout Cambridgeshire and other counties of England.

Externally, and particularly in the fourteenth century,

* Recently decorated in colour under the direction of Prof. Tristram.
† Although it is most unlikely that these are Mediaeval, they show, more clearly than any other examples from Cambridge, the character of fourteenth century label-stops.

carving was employed for those specialised parts of churches that gave opportunities for it—particularly on corbels—and to that century belong the 'ball-flower' (that superseded the dog-tooth) as an embellishment of such features as the ribs of spires, and a bolder treatment of the 'crocket'

Fig. 17. Wall tomb: manner of the fourteenth century.

or carved spur—first introduced in the thirteenth century—that became so prevalent in the fifteenth century. The wall-niche, richly treated—with buttresses, pinnacles and rib-vaulted ceiling, all in miniature (see Pl. V)—was introduced in the second quarter of the fourteenth century.

Fifteenth-century ('*Perpendicular*') *Gothic, Tudor and Early Renaissance.* Delicate work of the kind just described was carried out in the first half of the fifteenth century, but the latter half of that century saw the introduction of heraldic carving, which, though marked by a coarsening of execution in sculpture, was healthy, as, in the period roughly 1350 to 1450, there was a tendency to over-refinement in carving that sometimes amounted to finickiness. As a fourteenth century example of this tendency, readily observable, the interior of the Lady Chapel at Ely may be cited. Here, we can still see that the quality of the sculpture and carving is very high, but it lacks the robustness of the best work of the thirteenth century; though it should be remembered that it has lost practically all of the coloured finish that would have transformed it. Earlier and later fifteenth century work can be seen perfectly in King's College Chapel by comparing the internal wall treatment of the eastern portion—designed, and partly executed to the top of the windows, before 1450 —with that of the western portion carried out by Henry the Seventh, at the end of the fifteenth and very beginning of the sixteenth centuries.

At its best, the carving of the later fifteenth century in England, though tending to be formal, was fine and vigorous, as can be seen from Jesus College Gateway (Pl. XI), while there was a lot of its general feeling in much delightful localised work of the sixteenth, seventeenth and even early eighteenth centuries. A wooden bracket offered an opportunity that was rarely missed: a good example from the President's Lodge at Queens' College (Fig. 18), dating from about 1537, shows both Mediaeval and early Renaissance feeling. One of the finest examples in England of this carrying-on of the richness of late Mediaeval expression can be seen on the quadrangle side of the range leading to the garden at St John's College, Oxford, while another good early seventeenth century example, this time from Cambridge, is the west front of Peterhouse Chapel (Pl. XIV); but at this

29

stage we must walk warily, as Italian influences—later, ousted by German and Flemish ones—are apparent in work of the first half of the sixteenth century.

These influences are mainly discernible in carved ornament and (sparingly) painted decoration, as the finest carved

Queens' College
President's Lodge
Wood bracket
beneath overhang
of Gallery. c. 1537.

Fig. 18.

work of the earlier sixteenth century was inspired by, or directly produced by, Italian craftsmen; contrasting with the cruder work which succeeded it. In a kind of way, one sees in this a re-birth of the spirit of the 'Quattro Cento',★ that makes so much of this earlier carving peculiarly attractive; and we can find it most perfectly in Bishop West's

★ The fifteenth century in Italy. Its spirit is very noticeable in the 'Gate of Virtue' at Caius College, on the side shown in the Frontispiece to this book.

delightful stone Chapel at Ely Cathedral, finished in 1533:
the general design of this is not wholly late Mediaeval,
like the complementary Chapel of Bishop Alcock executed
in 1488; there are touches both in form and in delicate
carved enrichment that are of the early Renaissance, as also
are the plastered and painted
panels in the vaulted ceiling
(Fig. 19). Of carved woodwork by Italian artists, em-
bodied in a complete architectural treatment, Cam-
bridge has, perhaps, the finest
example in England in the
screen of King's College
Chapel, executed 1531–
1535, and therefore con-
temporary with the work at
Ely which has been cited.

Fig. 19. Ceiling panel, Bishop West's Chapel, Ely Cathedral, 1533.

Very different in character
from the preceding is the
output of contemporary large-scale heraldic work that was
used occasionally in the form of panels on the gatehouses of
the more important manors of the period. The manor house
of East Barsham, in Norfolk (c. 1525), shows one of the
best examples, the ornamental parts being carried out in
cut brick; but two Colleges in Cambridge—St John's and
Christ's—that had one Foundress in the first decade of the
sixteenth century, offered opportunities, that were not
missed, for this kind of work. Cambridge is indeed fortunate in possessing two such fine examples in stone, though
the slightly earlier carving inside and outside King's College
ante-chapel is greater in amount and well preserved; but the
College gateways come right into the street architecture
of the town and give it much distinction.

31

The most important works in Cambridge of the third quarter of the sixteenth century are Dr Caius's Gates at Caius College, to which reference has been made already (see above, p. 17); the 'Gate of Virtue' (see Frontispiece), which was earlier by some sixty-six years than Peterhouse Chapel, being surprisingly advanced, while its detail and ornament have a certain Classical grace.* The 'Gate of Honour' is coarser in treatment, though more out of the common. In its upper part, there is a grotesque head in the

Caius *Gate of Honour*

Fig. 20. 1569.

pediment, that is Italianesque, and Italian influence is plainly discernible in the three delicately-treated niches in shallow relief below the pediment; which, in view of what has been said about foreign influence in the sixteenth century, is not very remarkable, but the pattern of the carving on the heads of the splayed recesses in the lower part of the Gate (Fig. 20) is extraordinary. How, at that date, did this Romanized Mediterranean spiral pattern get there? Some pattern book from Italy getting into the hands of Dr Caius or his architect is the probable solution; and this may have contained some 'copy' from Diocletian's palace at Spalato or from an Early Christian mosaic.

Full Renaissance. As in Mediaeval architecture, so in Renaissance—and to a greater extent—there were decorative forms for the enrichment of cornices, architraves, etc. These were all based on usages of the Greeks of the fifth century B.C., worked by them with exquisite purity and a perfect

* Certainly, for its date, the most remarkable work in Cambridge. The side to Tree Court has the round arch; with its Corinthianesque capitals at the imposts and its victories in the spandrels, it might almost be a provincial work of the time of Hadrian; but the side to Caius Court is finer in style.

sense of the appropriate form for each kind of moulding; the 'egg and tongue' and the 'bead and reel' for larger and smaller rounded mouldings respectively, the 'leaf and tongue' for a wavy moulding or 'cyma reversa', and the console or carved bracket for door and window heads and (later) cornice projections; these being the principal set forms, while friezes, keystones and other members of a building were enriched with larger and less restricted ornament, or with sculpture.

The finest expressions in stone and wood of the Full Renaissance in England can be seen in the carved friezes, stone urns, etc. of such buildings as the Senate House (Pl. XXVI), the Old Schools (Pl. XXVII) and the Westmoreland Building at Emmanuel College (Pl. XXIV); and in the superlative wood-carving of such masters as Grinling Gibbons, which can be seen at Cambridge in some of the interior work in Trinity College Library.[4] At that time, also, English monumental sculpture had reached a very high level of excellence.

Plasterwork. From the later Middle Ages until the end of the eighteenth century, Plasterwork was an important factor in ornamental treatment. 'Parge-work', or the ornamenting of external walls that were plastered on timber framing, with simple patterns or coats of arms—modelled in relief and sometimes coloured—can be seen in the English country or in villages and towns, on sixteenth and seventeenth century buildings that are often quite humble; their internal ceilings sometimes being decorated in a similar way. Rooms of the more important buildings of the sixteenth century had finer ceilings, with moulded ribs set out in geometrical patterns; or plainer ribs with vine leaves and grapes in running bands, small enriched pendants and heraldry. A splendid example in Cambridge, dating from 1601, is in the Long Combination Room (formerly the Master's Lodge) of St John's College. This was the golden age of English oak panelling and of carved oak chimney-pieces and staircases, for domestic work, which can be seen—in conjunction with enriched plaster—not only in this fine room but in the rooms of other Cambridge Colleges.*

By 1630 these treatments had become bolder and more definitely schematic: shortly afterwards, large circular wreaths were used on ceilings, so that, in 1664, Wren was able to secure a largely-conceived and deeply-coved ceiling, with richly-panelled upper walls, all in plaster, in Pembroke College Chapel; the ante-chapel ceiling having one of the wreath treatments referred to above. A more lightly and freely treated ceiling, dating from 1690, can be seen in the Old Library of the same College. It should be noted, however, that after the end of the seventeenth century, plaster ceilings tended to be simpler, trusting for their effect on the formal moulded cornices of Georgian times. Later, what is now called the 'Adam's' style of plasterwork was more delicate, being based on the discovery by Robert Adam, about 1750, of low-relief plasterwork in or near Rome dating from the third and fourth centuries.

A word should be added about the use of *paint*. There can be no doubt that not only wall decoration in tempera paint (there were no 'easel pictures' in those days), but the embellishment of all internal forms by means of similar paint, was the ultimate expression aimed at in Mediaeval as in Greek work. To the Mediaeval as to the Greek mind, rough or dirty surfaces were an abomination; and so, when we see a Gothic vault in stone, we must imagine not only its richly carved bosses and its moulded ribs as painted and gilded, but the vault surfaces, as well as the wall surfaces below, coated with red or white on a ground of fine stucco (as in Greek stonework), relieved with pictures or patterns.[5]

* Pine began to replace oak for domestic woodwork about 1700.

There is some controversy about the extent to which colour was used for the embellishment of stonework after the latter part of the fifteenth century, and on enriched plaster ceilings of the late sixteenth and early seventeenth centuries, but there can be little doubt that the more important heraldic stone carving in the former category was coloured.

It might be thought that undue emphasis has been laid on Carving, Ornament and Decoration in this brief Introduction, but the subject is really important, though often relegated in histories of architecture to a few references or to a catalogic description: actually, ornament is one of the surest guides to style and, going even deeper, the nature of its use may be an indication of constructive tendencies. For example, the heavy exposed oak ceiling beams of the earlier sixteenth century gave opportunity for restricted spaces of plaster, easily capable of elaboration by a village craftsman; while, on the other hand, the more expansive plaster surfaces of ceilings in the later sixteenth century—when constructive elements tended to be hidden—offered new scope for the master-plasterer. Going further back, to Mediaeval times, we see the remarkable all-over treatment of Norman arches with large chevron or other patterns, that was superseded, at the end of the twelfth century, by the moulded arches of the Transitional period and the more elaborate undercut mouldings of the Early English period that followed it.[6] A mason, or school of masons, must have discovered the value of deeply-cut mouldings in an arch of recessed planes, and so this became the 'fashion'.[7] One has only to look at the arcading of the Early English Presbytery of Ely Cathedral—observing the delicacy of its dogtooth enrichment in arches that get their main emphasis by mouldings—and compare this with the wholly different Norman treatment of the Prior's door at Ely, or the chancel arch of Sturbridge Chapel, to realise the change.

In this concluding Section, it is advisable to clear the ground a little, as the terms *Renaissance* and *Modern*, in their archi-tectural applications, have been subject to various interpre-tations. The great historian of architecture, Fergusson, divided his work into two parts—the first, which he called a 'History of Architecture', ending with the Mediaeval styles; the second, which he called a 'History of Modern Architecture', beginning with Renaissance. It is perhaps safer to accept T. G. Jackson's definition—'The Renaissance of Roman Architecture', if only because the word 'Modern' is a dangerous one to use. It is sensible to talk of 'the archi-tecture of modern times', meaning by that, of our own times, but it is sometimes misleading to talk of 'modern archi-tecture'; and though it is now becoming a habit to use this term to define a particular expression of the present day, it is possible that future historians will call this 'the re-inforced concrete phase', when dealing with the twentieth century.

We can, however, use the word 'Modern' in archi-tecture, to define the periods after historic development had ceased; and it is usual, as well as being on the whole de-sirable, to include Renaissance as part of historic develop-ment. The true meaning of *Renaissance*, as opposed to *Revival*, is perhaps a matter of distinction rather than difference, but it is an important distinction: the Renaissance was a deep-rooted era of architectural development which spread through the whole of western Europe and lasted for at least 250 years, even in a country like England, where it began late and developed slowly; a Revival, on the other hand, has never been more than a comparatively short-lived phase.

As it has been mentioned that English Renaissance in-cluded the whole of the Georgian Age, this statement might be qualified here by the more accurate one that Renaissance ended in England during the last decade of the eighteenth century;[8] which, of course, would exclude *Regency* architecture; but that phase was to some extent eclectic, although, as generally understood, it was, in the main, Classic. It is really more important to realise the firmly-embedded Gothic tradition in English architecture, as something that was quite peculiar to England, and that resulted in our greatest nineteenth century building—the Houses of Parliament—being a purely Gothic structure. It has been pointed out that Inigo Jones's Banqueting House in Whitehall was built in 1621 in the purest Renaissance manner; several years earlier than Peterhouse Chapel, Clare College, and the Fellows' Building at Christ's College, which all have Mediaeval elements; while even as late as the second decade of the eighteenth century, Wren was building Gothic church towers in London. Gothic 'dilettantism' (as it should be called at that stage) was in full evidence in Horace Walpole's 'Strawberry Hill', begun in 1753, and some ten years earlier, Batty Langley had published *Gothick Architecture Improved*; so that, at the most, we can only see a period of some twenty years in the first half of the eighteenth century, when mediaevalism—in some form or another—was not apparent in England; for, needless to say, it persisted into the nineteenth century. Such a short period as this can be discounted altogether, as any observant person can see that in the depths of the English countryside, the village craftsman—right through the eighteenth century—never abandoned some of the Gothic tricks of his forefathers.

THE GOTHIC REVIVAL AND THE CLASSIC REVIVAL

These generalised remarks are, perhaps, more important for the present purpose than any attempt at a reasoned account of nineteenth century architecture, obviously too large a subject to discuss here; while, in this book, only two Plates have been allotted to that century. These Plates emphasise its two outstanding stylistic phases, the Gothic and the Classic Revivals, both of which belong to the first half of the century; though the Gothic Revival was more persistent, largely on account of its weighty ecclesiastical background. To show how each was dependent on the

Fig. 21. Downing College; south-west Pavilion: William Wilkins, 1818.

'fashion' encouraged by a particular clique, we can note the remarkable fact that Savage's St Luke's Church, Chelsea—a pure Gothic structure—and Inwood's St Pancras Church —a pure Greek Revival structure—were built at precisely the same time, in 1819–20.

The 'Classic' Revival was, in fact, a 'Greek' Revival to a very large extent; and here it should be noted that though this movement can be seen in contemporary France and

Germany, it was England that led the way: at least four of the principal architects concerned with the Classic Revival in England during the first half of the nineteenth century—Stuart, Inwood, Wilkins and Cockerell—had made intensive first-hand study of Greek remains; and the work of Wilkins and Cockerell, in particular, was endued with a fine feeling for form and detail—see Fig. 21.

THE LATER NINETEENTH AND EARLY TWENTIETH CENTURIES

Cambridge can show a considerable amount of architectural work—some of it distinguished—that belongs to the times that can definitely be termed 'Modern'; a proportion of which shows later variations of the Gothic Revival.[9] It has been thought advisable to include an example from the present century, as being more significant to the student of to-day, and the reader can be referred to the description of Plate XXXI for information about it. All that need be added here is that the architecture of the nineteenth century in England—much as it has been decried—deserves its book, and it is to be hoped that, some day, it will have it.

1, p. 9. The cusp, or meeting point of adjacent foliations in tracery, etc. (see Figs 3, 4 and 6), might perhaps be called the most significant feature of Gothic architecture; it is certainly the one on which three-fourths of the elaboration of Gothic window tracery depends. It was used in early Moslem work at Samarra (Iraq) and Cordova (in the form of multifoil arches) in the ninth century.

2, p. 13. The moulded bands on Early English shafts (see Fig. 9) were utilitarian in origin, as they were necessary to stiffen these long thin members by connecting them to the wall, or to the core of a pier. Purbeck marble was the usual material for these shafts: in the arcading of the Presbytery of Ely Cathedral, not only the shafts with their moulded bands, but the core and entire moulded and carved capital of each pier, are of Purbeck, having its fine natural grey polish; which is unusual. No other building in England offers such splendid opportunities for a study of the varied uses of this material as Ely Cathedral: the Presbytery piers are the poetry of fine masonry.

3, p. 23. The employment of an Order overriding height defini-tion by storeys was a favourite device of Palladio, in the sixteenth century, though he was not the first Italian architect to adopt a treatment which originated in late Classical times; but the term 'Palladian' has stuck, and 'Palladianism' means, more than any-thing else, the use of these gigantic Orders.

4, p. 33. Carvers and sculptors—the names are often indifferently applied to the same person—worked alike in relief and in the round; an example of Gibbons's skill in combining high and low relief may be seen in his fine wall-monument to Robert Cotton, in Conington church, south of the Huntingdon road, about ten miles from Cambridge.*

5, p. 34. Some churches within a few miles of Cambridge show good examples of wall-painting, recovered recently. The best single figure is the St Agnes (fourteenth century) at Willingham,

* I am indebted to Mrs K. A. Esdaile for the greater part of this note. For the treatment of the whole subject, see her book, *English Monumental Sculpture since the Renaissance* (S.P.C.K., 1927).

but Kingston has a complete scheme over the chancel arch—a cross and angels, etc. in white on a red ground, dating from the end of the fourteenth century.

6, p. 35. Norman arches were, at most, very simply moulded when unadorned; and when so found, border on Transitional with its first use of the pointed arch. An example of late Norman moulded arcading can be seen in the north transept of Christ Church Cathedral, Oxford, interesting to compare with the slightly later pointed Transitional arches of the crossing in Jesus College Chapel, Cambridge, with their fine use of the dog-tooth (see p. 26 and Glossary).

7, p. 35. Fashion, in a living age of architectural discovery, is a synonym for change of style as a continuous and understandable progressive process. In modern times, a significant European 'fashion' that the future historian of architecture will be able to record, is the interesting phase of the last decade of the nineteenth century known as 'l'Art Nouveau'; which, though short-lived as a general expression, has not received the attention it deserves, as its processes are still discernible.

8, p. 37. The statement in the *Encyclopaedia Britannica* (14th edition, 'Renaissance') that Sir William Chambers (died 1796) and Robert Adam (died 1792) were the last great architects of the English Renaissance, may be accepted as substantially correct.

9, p. 39. See the description to Plate XXIX. As an example of the earlier Gothic Revival, equal in importance to Wilkins's work at Corpus Christi College, Cambridge possesses the New Court of St John's College—including a bridge over the river—that has considerable romantic qualities. It was designed by Rickman and Hutchinson in 1826.

PLATES

and

DESCRIPTIONS

*Figures (e.g. Fig. 1 a) mentioned in the Descriptions,
refer to text illustrations in the Introduction.*

Saxon Arch – St. Benet's. Cambridge.   RWS 1918.

TOWER ARCH

Saxon Romanesque　　　　　　　　　　*Late 10th Century*
Stone

Cambridge is fortunate in possessing this noble Arch, a work of major importance belonging to the later Saxon period, dating, probably, from near the end of the tenth century. It has the outstanding characteristics of fully-developed Saxon work—the broad, plain semicircular (or slightly flattened semicircular) main arch, surmounted by a moulded outer-ring; the well-defined impost mouldings at the springing of the arch with their 'returned' projections to take the moulded arch-ring above; the continuation of this element down the wall by projecting strip-pilasters; and the 'long and short' treatment of these and of the plain stone jambs. Where this Cambridge arch has special distinction is in the reclining beast sculptures above the imposts, a feature rare in itself, but, where present, emphasising the underlying sculptural idea that was present in the finest Saxon work. It can be seen how, in this case, the sculptural element lifts the whole design out of the range of ordinary building.

The impost mouldings are of a type that is met with in late Roman and Early Christian buildings in the Near East, while the treatment of the arch proper closely resembles Etruscan examples of the third century B.C.; the strip-pilasters being an early Romanesque feature, again originating directly—in all probability —from Syrian work of the third and fourth centuries of our era, but with a much earlier derivation from Mesopotamia. The base stones are modern, but the rest of the work is preserved in its Saxon integrity, though without the smooth finish it may have had once: it is at any rate clear that the recessed small rough stones between the jambs and the strip-pilasters were originally covered with plaster, finished with fine stucco to the same face as the dressed stonework.

45

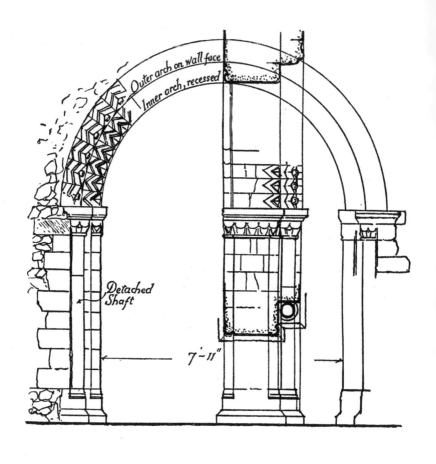

Outer arch on wall face
Inner arch, recessed

Detached
Shaft

7'-11"

Stourbridge Chapel
Cambridge
The Chancel Arch

12 6 0 1 2 3 4 5 6 7 8

THE CHANCEL ARCH

Norman Romanesque   *12th Century*

Stone

Cambridge has a rare example of twelfth century Norman architecture in the 'Round Church', but the fine chancel arch of the
little 'Leper' Chapel, beside Barnwell railway station, on the
Newmarket side of the town—of which an elevation, section and
part plan are shown—is more useful to illustrate the methods of
Norman builders in work of a decorative kind. It is interesting to
compare this arch with that of the previous illustration, as we can
see that the long and short work and the strip-pilasters of the jambs
have disappeared, and that the arch itself is carved with the chevron
or 'zig-zag'; this being the method of decoration most favoured by
Norman builders: two methods of working it are exhibited in the
Plate and in Fig. 1 *a*.

Ornament of this kind may have begun with painted decoration,
but the Norman masons saw in it an opportunity for rounding-off
and embellishing the recessed planes of their arches; for, in contradistinction to Saxon work, each succeeding ring of a Norman arch
projected beyond the one below it; hence the term 'recessed' (or
'receding') planes. At Sturbridge we see two arch-rings: sometimes there were more. We see also that each jamb has the
detached shaft which was carried into thirteenth century work,
and that the capitals at the imposts are of 'cubical' form with the
square abaci that are present without exception in Norman
Romanesque; the masons having enriched these capitals with subsidiary mouldings and patterns without losing their essential form
(see Fig. 1 *a*).

The Chapel is all that remains of the twelfth century Leper
Hospital at Sturbridge. It retains all its original character to a
remarkable extent, and has now, fortunately, been put into use
again.

octagonal

round →

1'–10"

WINDOW ON SOUTH SIDE

Norman Romanesque   *12th Century*
Stone

Continuing with this interesting little building, the Plate shows the exterior of a window and part of the walling on the south side. Equally with Plate II, this illustrates Norman methods of expression that were applicable, also, to more important forms of the period, such as the pier arches of naves in large churches or cathedrals; for the style was pre-eminently one in which decorative enrichment of a formal kind was used extensively on structural members in a building. Occasionally, as on the west front of Castle Rising Church in Norfolk—where we find windows with interlaced arches supporting a larger central window, all elaborately ornamented, and a doorway with carved arches below— this enrichment dominates an entire façade.* At Sturbridge Chapel we find the same ideas concentrated on separate features: of these the window shown here is outstanding.

Each stone of the outer arched head is carved with a chevron, varying slightly in treatment from those on the chancel arch; the recessed arched head of the window being in one stone, with some rough patterns on it in low relief, evidently done in a haphazard way by the mason to amuse himself. The very interesting shaft on the left is, fortunately, well-preserved: it has two versions of zig-zag carving to imitate marble veining, but near the centre the square form of the shaft stone is retained and circular carved discs have been worked on it. The shafts carry the usual cubical capitals —surmounted by plain heavy impost stones in place of moulded abaci—the one on the right being the better preserved. The worked string-course, on which the window stands, runs round the whole building and is illustrated more fully in Fig. 1 *d*; *e* in the same figure showing the base of the shaft, while *b* and *c* show patterns on other window arches of the Chapel.

Norman work on a much grander scale than anything in this building, though not so fully enriched, can be seen at Ely Cathedral.

* J. S. Cotman made a fine drawing of this, reproduced in Budden's *English Gothic Churches.*

East End of Jesus Coll. Chapel. Cambridge - EH 1928

THE CHAPEL

Early English Gothic   *First Half of* 13th Century
Stone

The Chapel proper at Jesus College, the eastern end of which is shown here, was originally part of the presbytery or choir of the thirteenth century conventual church of St Radegund, and therefore the oldest building in Cambridge used as a College Chapel. It is a gem of the 'Early English' or thirteenth century period of English Gothic. Though small, it exhibits the finest characteristics of that period. We can see these in the strong nervous lines of the shafting, which, on the north wall, run right down to the floor (on the south wall the sedilia prevent this and necessitate a raising of the window-sills), and in the beautiful arcaded design of the upper eastern wall, forming a rich frame for the austere simplicity of the three tall lancets with their deep plain reveals.★ As usual in Early English treatments the sill-tables of the window groups form continuous string-courses at fairly high levels, and the height of the shafting is relieved by moulded bands, the lower bands of the north wall shafting being in line with, and a variant of, the sill-table mouldings (see Fig. 9). The mouldings throughout show the deep undercutting that prevailed in Early Gothic work.

The side walls are actual thirteenth century work. The east wall is supremely good restoration by Augustus Welby Pugin, carried out from existing evidences to the top of the lancet windows in 1846–47. The cinquefoil window and the blind quatrefoil roundels on each side of it, by Pugin, are entirely in character and are most valuable to the design. The roof was also re-constructed by Pugin in place of the flat ceiling put in at the end of the eighteenth century.

★ Another good Early English treatment with three lancets at Cambridge can be seen in the 'Abbey Church' (the parish church of Barnwell Priory), on the north side of Newmarket Road. A sketch of one of the window heads is shown in Fig. 2.

St Mary the Less, Cambridge - 8th Feb 1929

Decorated Gothic   *Mid-14th Century*
        Stone

This church—formerly used by Peterhouse as a Chapel—is the
most representative example in Cambridge of English 'Decorated'
Gothic architecture; this, at its best, being not later than 1349,
the date of the 'Black Death'. The church is without aisles, and
the tall side walls show to advantage a main characteristic of the
ecclesiastical buildings of the period—the introduction of large
windows with the elaborate 'flowing' tracery that became the
highest technical achievement of English masons in such work.

In the splendid windows that are of fourteenth century date
(1340–1352)—i.e. the eight four-light ones on the side walls (see
Fig. 3) and the six-light one on the east wall—the main controlling lines can be clearly seen, and though the patterns of the
tracery seem intricate on account of their cusped projections, they
have admirable balance. The central mullion of each window,
which has the most weight to take, is slightly thicker than the
others, and the mouldings express this quite logically; while it will
be seen, on careful observation, that a fine simplicity is produced,
as the junction of the outermost moulded surface with the wall in
each window is a single and uninterrupted line from the sill-table
to the apex of the arch.

The canopied niche on each side of the east window is a fourteenth century feature that was continued into the fifteenth
century, highly significant as showing a formal placing of decorative elements not met with in the thirteenth century.* Though
the church is buttressed externally, it is clear that the original roof
was of wood; stone vaulting being very rarely used except in
cathedrals and the large monastic churches. The west end contains,
at the entrance, elements of an original twelfth century building,
and immediately east of this there was some mid-fifteenth
century re-building: of this, a 'Perpendicular' window-head is
shown in Fig. 4.

* The statues on pedestals in these niches are modern.

THE OLD COURT

Decorated Gothic	*Late 14th Century*
Rubble stone with stuccoed finish and worked stone dressings	*with later Mediaeval and Modern adaptations*

The Old Court of the College is of very special interest, as it shows the semi-domestic side of architecture in the fourteenth century; being the only example, in either University, of a College court which preserves the feeling of that early period; while its later Mediaeval elements do not come into the picture on the first impression we get of this quiet secluded enclosure, in which we seem to lose all sense of time.

It is impossible to analyse the *design* architecturally, as its qualities have grown in a particularly happy way from the fourteenth till the beginning of the twentieth century; but the main values consist of the earliest elements and the sympathetic handling of the Court by a modern architect*—who knew and loved both Cambridge and his College—with a healthy and unbiased respect for tradition, that produced, without copyism, new things that were harmonious. The Court was literally 'tidied-up', but its charm and essential domesticity were preserved, and even strengthened; for mediaeval decay, though not without qualities in a ruin, should have no place in a used building.

There is every reason to believe that the roofs were originally finished with projecting eaves, as at present, and not against upstanding battlements. The buttresses and the pointed doors and windows on the ground storey belong to the earliest building, while two fifteenth century windows can be seen in the upper storey; Barnack stone being used for the buttresses, and clunch for the remainder of the stonework. The Saxon tower of St Bene't's Church, just appearing at the right top corner of the picture, forms an effective object in the background on the north side of the Court.

* Mr T. H. Lyon.

FROM SOUTH-EAST (BOTOLPH LANE)

Perpendicular Gothic

Small-stone rubble and dressed stone

Second Quarter of 15th Century

England is celebrated for the number and excellence of its church towers, due very largely to the great activity in church building during the fifteenth century. In Saxon and Norman times buttresses were either absent or had very slight projection; but the later towers were buttressed, because even small churches adopted the structural type of large and important ones that required buttresses to absorb the thrusts of vault springers or roof trusses, the walls between becoming thinner; so that buttressing became a universal practice, and it should be borne in mind that the first stage of a tower was often roofed with a groined vault in stone.

The obvious function of the tower as a bell chamber necessitated a staircase in one corner giving access to the bell frame, and the staircase turret gave character to the whole structure; usually being carried to the top of the tower for access to the tower roof, and occasionally, as here, being buttressed. The corners of towers were often surmounted by pinnacles, but at St Botolph's, in place of these, there are upstanding stone sculptures, now so much worn that it is difficult to understand their meaning.*

Other unusual features at St Botolph's are the lintelled outer definition of the two-light windows in the top stage of the tower, and the south porch forming a stop-end to the south chantry chapel. The fine handling of the south-east angle of the tower, below the top stage, to enable its east face to take the full span of the nave roof, is worth careful note. Many East Anglian churches, like this one, were built of flint or small-stone rubble with dressed stone in important positions, the rubble being covered with a coat of rough lime plastering, leaving only the dressed stonework exposed.

* Though careful examination makes it practically certain that they are the symbols of the Evangelists, the mitre or headgear given to each has led many to think that they are statues of Saints or Doctors of the Catholic Church.

THE CHAPEL, SOUTH SIDE

Perpendicular Gothic   1446 *to* 1515

Stone

King's College Chapel illustrates, on a grand scale, Gothic principles in their latest or 'Perpendicular' phase, as well as any building can. It is one of a group of Chapels of Royal Foundation belonging to the reigns of Henry the Sixth and Henry the Seventh; of these the sister Chapel at Eton resembles it most nearly, and these two are almost contemporary as Foundations of Henry the Sixth; the others being St George's Chapel, Windsor, and Henry the Seventh's Chapel at Westminster Abbey. King's is the largest of the four—it is about the same length as Wells Cathedral without its Lady Chapel and the parapets of the side walls are ninety-five feet above the ground—but it has still greater distinction in the preservation of its early sixteenth century glass; and its incomparable interior, making it, perhaps, the finest Chapel in the world, is the glory of Cambridge.

The exterior is impressive for its sheer mass, its height, and the awe-inspiring area of the great windows. It has monumental character but also great decorative quality, as the richness in the upper parts of the beautifully-designed corner turrets is continued by the pinnacles which surmount the buttresses, the finely-patterned effect of the parapets and the rich carving on the buttress fronts. The view emphasises the cliff-like character of the Chapel and shows the south side in such sharp perspective that the great windows, owing to the depth of the buttresses, are invisible. Though vertical quality is outstanding, there is a pronounced horizontal element in the enriched cresting of the range of side chapels and the continuous base-mouldings of the building. All the carving, as usual in Perpendicular work, is markedly heraldic and formal. The four turrets are arresting in any distant view of Cambridge.

ENTRANCE GATEWAY

Tudor, with earlier and   *Late 14th or 15th to*
    later elements   *16th Century*
        Stone

Pembroke College shows the only example of a Cambridge Gateway emphasised by two oriels and central heraldic carving on the upper storey, and this is a form that may be earlier in its origin than the turreted-tower, early sixteenth century form, of which there are examples in Cambridge—at Queens', Christ's, St John's and Trinity Colleges; but at Pembroke the upper storey is Elizabethan and dates, in all probability, from the third quarter of the sixteenth century.

The treatment of the oriels is vigorous and effective, recalling the very fine and slightly earlier ones—that have pointed windows—on the garden front of St John's College, Oxford, where the doorway below the oriel is early seventeenth century Renaissance. At Pembroke, Cambridge, on the other hand, the actual Gateway is of fifteenth century Gothic form, and may have been built at that time or even earlier; as, in this part of the College, there are remains of the original clunch walling that date from the Foundation in the middle of the fourteenth century.

Practically the whole of this front of the College was refaced in modern times: we can now see only general idea and character with little original work; but we can appreciate the original design motive, which is very satisfactory. The Gateway itself, in its plain wall, gains dignity from the balanced oriels above, centralised by the boldly-carved decorative feature that fills the space between them; while the semi-domestic character pertaining properly to collegiate work is secured by the tiled roof and the dormer windows of the attic.

61

CLOISTER COURT, WEST RANGE

Late Perpendicular   *Third Quarter of*
Brick and Stone   *15th Century*

Queens' College shares, with St John's, the distinction of having a great part of its brickwork in its original state, and these two are the great exemplars of the brick-built college; but Queens' is the earlier, and it still has much work that belongs to the time of its first Royal Foundress,* who commenced her buildings just before the middle of the fifteenth century. No visitor to Cambridge should fail to observe the original part of its south side in Silver Street, where Mediaeval brickwork can be seen of a quality that is unsurpassed in England, or even in Europe.

The whole College has a delightful atmosphere, though it is comparatively small, as it was, of necessity, overshadowed by the great Foundation that Henry the Sixth was accomplishing at King's; but it shows some extremely interesting forms, and, in particular, the square angle-turrets of the buildings around the principal Court, of a kind that Henry intended to embody in his own College. The Gateway, with turrets that have diminishing stages, is the earliest of its type in Cambridge, and there is a beautiful fifteenth century door of carved oak in the 'Screens'.

The west range of the Cloister Court is one of the original parts of the College, and its widely-spaced late Gothic stone windows, with their deep outer arches of plain brick (see also Fig. 5), are characteristic of the period; as are the Cloister 'panes' and doors, built with splayed bricks in recessed planes, and with flattened arches that are just pointed. The clear division into storeys, and the rhythmical association of the upper and lower openings, make the whole front an object lesson in treatment; while the tiled roof —with eaves instead of an embattled parapet—and the continuous stone drip-course below the windows, give a feeling of quiet domesticity to the whole. On the right, part of the sixteenth century half-timbered front of the President's Lodge can be seen.

* Margaret of Anjou, Queen of Henry the Sixth.

Late Perpendicular   *Bishop Alcock, Founder*
Brick and Stone   *c.* 1498

The Gateway of the Founder is the only example in Cambridge
of this feature as a square tower without angle-turrets, and there
is no doubt that it shows the original design in all essentials; and
although it was barbarously pulled about in 1791, it was very
skilfully restored in 1880. We see in it the formal elements—such
as the canopied niches on the east wall of the Church of St Mary
the Less (Pl. V)—which began in Gothic architecture about the
middle of the fourteenth century; but in later times these were
intensified, producing, in this fine work, so many rhythms that
the result might almost be called 'Gothic Baroque'.

As in most Perpendicular or early Tudor Gateways, the central
motive is the splendid crocketed finial proceeding from the
crocketed label-mouldings of the doorway, that forms, with
the statue of the bishop in his canopied niche, an exceptionally tall
decorative spine reaching nearly to the topmost stage of the tower.
Woven into all this are the contrasted steppings—one downward
the other upward—of the string-courses that mark the diminishing stages of the tower.

The whole of these elements are brought into gravity and restraint by the four two-light windows, but the stone crosses beside
the upper windows give lateral expansion just where it is needed,
in contrast to the binding quality of the heavily-moulded entry
and the pinnacled shaftings which rise from its sides. The design
would stand complete without the pronounced crenellations of the
topmost stage, but these give it additional lift and dignity. The
'inband' and 'outband' stone quoins, running from the top to
the lowest string-course, frame a composition which is one of the
most striking pieces of design in the whole range of the later
Mediaeval architecture of England; though the effect of the tower
would, no doubt, have been considerably increased when the
flanking buildings were in their original state, at a lower level than
they are at present.

FIRST COURT, WEST RANGE

Mostly Early Tudor   1510–1516

Brick and Stone   *with later elements*

St John's College, excepting its New Buildings on the other side of the river, is built entirely of brick, with only certain dressings and special features of stone; and, being very large, it is also the only College in Cambridge which has three courts, all of considerable size, opening in direct succession from one another.

The Second Court is usually considered the most interesting, because it has remained practically untouched since it was built; but a court in this position, unless it is particularly arresting in its treatment, can hardly have the general interest of a First Court, which can be seen through a fine Gateway from the street. Although the First Court does not possess the unity of the Second Court—its north side being entirely occupied by the new Chapel built in 1864—the view in the Plate shows how attractive some of its features are, while this west range is also a good example of a central treatment which binds together successfully elements that might have been ineffective in combination; consisting, in this case, of the Hall on the right and the Rooms on the left.

The fine Tudor doorway in stone, standing well on steps leading to the 'Screens', contrasts most admirably with the equally good late seventeenth century stone niche of baroque character, with its sculpture, which is placed above it; and this latter feature in particular, by its association with the enriched horizontal element of the embattled parapet and the string-course, gives great value to the whole composition—though the effective brick patterns have become less evident since the recent cleaning of the walls—while the necessary vertical emphasis is provided by the buttresses and the old lead rainwater pipes in their prepared positions.

Early and Late Tudor   *Great Gate*, 1519–1535

Stone, and Brick and Stone   *Fountain*, 1602

Great Court, Trinity, is not only the biggest thing of its kind in Oxford or Cambridge, but is, perhaps, the largest enclosed court-yard in Europe. King's is the only other College in Cambridge that has a centrally-placed monument in its principal Court, but the Fountain at Trinity is not Modern; it is one of the important features of the strong late-Elizabethan element which Ralph Nevile imparted to the College, and it should be studied in conjunction with the doorway to the 'Screens' from Great Court, with Nevile's Court, and with Nevile's Gate at the end of Trinity Lane.

The Fountain is, perhaps, the finest thing of its kind in England, standing with great distinction in its wide surroundings and having the vigour and decorative quality of the best work of its time. Though it was put together again on its present stepped base in comparatively recent times, it still preserves all its essential qualities, embodying an established type for this kind of structure, of which Cambridge fortunately possesses another example— smaller and less splendid, but full of interest—in 'Hobson's Conduit', erected in the Market in 1614.*

The view, taken from the 'Screens', is only one of many fine views in this Court, but it has the advantage of showing Great Gate in the background, and Great Gate is again the biggest thing of its kind in Oxford or Cambridge; an example, with truly monu-mental proportions, of the four-turreted gatehouse tower. It is built of brick with a sparing use of stone, as were the similarly-built structures from the time of Henry the Eighth with which it was in relation; and the stone re-facings and parapets of these buildings—carried out during the seventeenth century and later— retained a few of the window surrounds, while the roofs still have their original form.†

* Since 1855 it has been in its present position at the corner of Lensfield Road and Trumpington Road.

† The walling north of the Gate was refaced again in 1936. There is a small length of the original brick walling of the east range, immediately adjoining the Gate to the south, but on its street side. We can see there, also, the simple form of the original eaves, without a parapet.

PETERHOUSE XIV
THE CHAPEL: WEST FRONT

Early Stuart   *Doctor Matthew Wren*
Immature Renaissance   *c.* 1633
Stone

This is one of the most interesting examples in Cambridge of the change-over from Gothic to Renaissance. It is instructive to compare it—and the nearly similar east front—with those by Dr Caius for the 'Gate of Virtue' at Gonville and Caius College, which were built some sixty-six years earlier and were admittedly advanced for their date; though it should be borne in mind that the pronounced Mediaeval features in the Chapel west front—the window, the niches on each side of it, and the door—indicate the greater tendency towards Gothic in ecclesiastical buildings. The Gate itself at Caius, on its 'Tree Court' side, has the Renaissance round arch; on its 'Caius Court' side (see Frontispiece) it has the pseudo-Tudor arch, classically detailed, which can be seen in the Peterhouse arcading, although there also the round arch was used on each side of the Chapel front. All this proves how difficult it is to date accurately English buildings of the Immature Renaissance type.

The west front treatment at Peterhouse is essentially one for a collegiate court, repeated in a different manner by Sir Christopher Wren at Emmanuel College (Pl. XVIII), but the details at Peterhouse show all sorts of curious tricks: the niches, though Mediaeval in principle and in much of their decoration, have the scalloped-shell heads of the Classical tradition, while other elements suggest a set-piece of furniture.* The carefully-designed corner pilaster features are linked up with the vigorous ramps and hollows of the gable, a Dutch-inspired treatment that carries the eye up to the squared portion above and to the ultimate decorative feature.

The strapwork in relief on the plinth and pedestals at the base of the building is a typical Jacobean form of decoration, and the emphasis given to the ashlar facing of the wall by gentle rustication, stamps the whole work as more Renaissance than Mediaeval.†

* The ball and spike finishes, seen here, persisted in grandfather clocks till well into the eighteenth century.
† Mr H. C. Hughes considers that on the east front and exposed side portions of the Chapel a brick and stone treatment was intended, though not carried out.

71

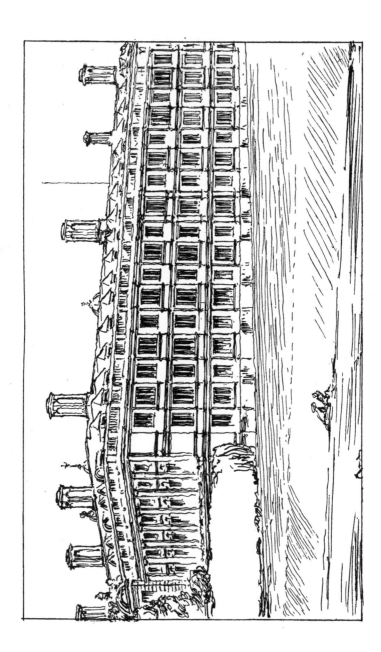

FROM KING'S COLLEGE BRIDGE

Early and Full Renaissance   South Front, 1640

Stone   West Front, 1669–1715

Clare, seen at an angle from the river, is the most striking example of a collegiate building that stands in the open, either at Oxford or Cambridge, while it gives most of the story of English architecture, from late Gothic till the maturity of eighteenth century Renaissance. It is fortunate that, except for its Chapel, Clare was designed and built almost entirely by the Grumbold family of builders, as the various changes and additions they effected during seventy-six years did not disturb continuity in design; the most important changes in the south front being the substitution of square-headed windows for pointed ones and of a balustraded parapet for a battlemented one.

The character of the building from this south-west aspect is peculiarly happy. The quiet rhythmical breaks in the wall treatment of the south front are reposeful and counteract any tendency to monotony, and the fact that these have achieved a perfect balance between horizontal and vertical elements is worthy of close attention. The pilaster treatment of the west or river front is so gentle that it appears almost accidental, yet it gives richness and vertical emphasis that act as a foil to the horizontal lines of the river and the bridge. The windows of this front—carrying pediments on the main floor—show the change-over to Full Renaissance in their classically-moulded architraves and their barred sash-frames.

The building owes much to the regular recurrence of bold but finely-designed dormers in the roof and to the massive stone chimney-stacks designed with equal care.

IVY COURT, SOUTH SIDE

Stuart   1658–1661

Brick and Stone

This, the original 'New Court' of Pembroke College, entered through the 'Screens', discloses a problem of architectural treatment at its eastern end. Nearly two-thirds of this is only separated from the Fellows' Garden* by a wall with an interesting gateway removed from the west end of the 'Screens' of the Old Hall; the remaining part of this end, that was built up about thirty years ago, being admittedly a difficult essay for any architect. The buildings on the north and south sides of the Court, however, are able to hold their own because of the quiet consistency of their general effect, though there is a remarkable architectural history behind them. Recent research makes it probable that the portion of the south range that has the tall pedimented feature—shown on the right of the sketch—was, notwithstanding appearances, built (in 1658) *before* the remainder of the range in 1661; at that date the late Mediaeval character of the north range of the Court— the greater part of which was built in 1614–1617—appealed more to a new governing body in the College.†

The whole Court is an object lesson in the change-over period from Mediaeval to Renaissance, and the south front is full of architectural interest. The roof treatment, with its fine gabled dormer windows surmounted by ball-finials (see Fig. 12), and with the smaller dormer windows of the garrets at a higher level,‡ is, in its way, unequalled in Cambridge; while the value of the round-headed stone doorways, in giving unified character to the composition as a whole, is noteworthy. It will be seen, also, that the double row of dormers is fully able to balance the stone pedimented motive with its flanking dormers that are more classically-inspired than the others. The elements that are notably Mediaeval are the mullioned windows without transoms, though their mouldings show the new influence of the time.

* This has always been a garden since 1363, when the Foundress purchased it.
† See *A Short History of Pembroke College, Cambridge*, by Aubrey Attwater, pp. 73, 76 and 79 (Cambridge University Press, 1936).
‡ These garrets were occupied by college servants till the later years of the nineteenth century.

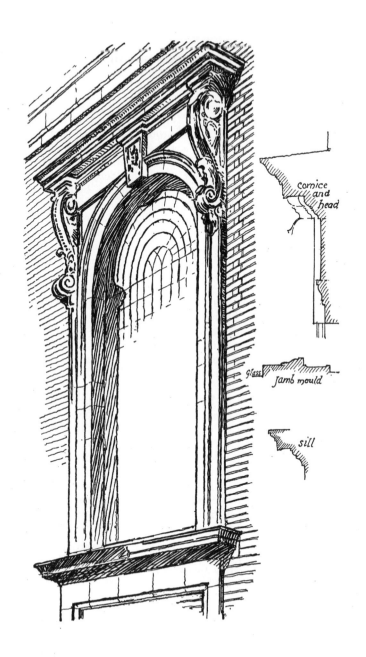

cornice
and
head

glass jamb mould

sill

Full Renaissance   *Sir Christopher Wren*
Brick and Stone   1663–1664

Pembroke College Chapel, probably the first authentic building by Wren, is not only a fine piece of architecture, but is remarkable for the early adoption of a type of design which Wren made peculiarly his own, and which he continued to use till the end of his days; so that the window shown here does not differ materially from those in many of the City churches of his mature period. Wren's brickwork, when used with stone, is impressive because of its broad value as carefully-built walling, and the stone elements are introduced with a measure of intelligence that we find in the work of no other English architect.

There can be no question that this window has value as a decorative feature, but the stone treatment of which it forms the principal part is not merely a window; it is something which reaches from the base of the building well up towards the top, and the great panel is just as typical of Wren's methods in design. The window has an archivolt moulding that is continuous with those of the jambs, a treatment found in Italian early Renaissance buildings, and one which Wren was fond of using; further, the consoles are contained exactly in the width of the panelled stone uprights that are outside the jamb mouldings, so that the most important practical considerations—the form of the daylight opening for the glazing and the meeting of the brickwork and the stonework—are both achieved satisfactorily. Mastery can be seen in the handling as well as the form, the mouldings being typical of those that the great architect used throughout his career, as he was remarkably consistent in his treatment of Renaissance, and a design by him can nearly always be recognised.

A small but very careful model in wood was prepared for Pembroke Chapel, and there was little deviation from this in essentials when the building was carried out, though the present Sanctuary is an addition of the later nineteenth century;* the design and material of the original east end being retained externally.

* By G. G. Scott, the Younger: a fine and sympathetic work.

77

THE CHAPEL

Full Renaissance

Stone

Sir Christopher Wren

1665–1667

All Wren's work in Cambridge bears the undoubted stamp of his genius. This early example, built certainly from drawings by him, is comparatively small, but, as the view shows, has monumental quality and a proper regard for the emphasis of essentials. The quietness of the secondary motive—the continuous line of the cloister, the panelled band and the windowed gallery above—is not disturbed unduly by the end of the Chapel; yet the latter takes its place with easy dignity as the main motive of the design. Whenever he could dispense with them Wren avoided pedestals under main columns or pilasters, and here the bases of these stand directly on the pavement and take up the alignment of the plain bases of the cloister piers.

Richness is concentrated on the upper part of the Chapel front, beginning with the splendid treatment of the sub-frieze between the Corinthian capitals; the clock being beautifully set as a really adequate centrepiece, balanced by the scrolled ends, the finials, and the accessory carving of the split-pediment.* The lantern, as always in Wren's designs, is fully adequate as a crowning feature to the whole composition, while the carved members in the arcade below introduce a quiet element of enrichment that is in sympathy with the pediment treatment. Here we can see to perfection what the Renaissance could achieve when handled by a master.

The provision of pavilion roofs to the two sides of the range enabled the upper side walls of the Chapel to run straight back uninterruptedly, producing an element of lightness that is invaluable to a composition firmly anchored to the ground by the Order in the centre; so that full static quality is obtained, necessary to balance the strong rhythmic feeling of the arcade.

* See note to Pl. XXI.

THE OLD GATES

Full Renaissance   *c.* 1671

Stone

These are the finest gates in Cambridge, forming a noble bridge-head to the old approach from the 'Backs', though the vista beyond, on the east side, is hardly worthy of them. From the College they can be reached by a side entry in the Third Court. Bridge and Gates must have been constructed together as they form an organic whole; while the unusual height and depth of the abutment afforded by the parapets of a bridge gave an opportunity for monumental treatment of which full advantage was taken, resulting in a conception that is splendidly decorative and big in scale.

The motive of each pier—a simple square form panelled on the face, standing on a pedestal and topped by a boldly-projecting cornice, which is surmounted by a rampant beast bearing an armorial shield—is characteristic of the period; as also is the pilaster strip on the inner face, finished on the top with a console, an idea both practically and aesthetically sound. The architectural details are carried out with great delicacy, the heraldic relief-carving on the piers is finely and expressively executed, and the heraldic sculptures on their raised ornamental bases are a fitting completion of the whole design.

These Gates are the largest in Cambridge, the piers being over seventeen feet high to the top of the cornice, and three feet six inches wide on the face; this width being evidently a standard one for gate piers, as those on the St John's Backs and at St Catharine's are almost exactly similar in that respect. The wrought-iron gates, having an excellent overthrow,* are good work of the early eighteenth century.

* Ornamental ironwork, above and attached to, the fixed top bars of tall gates.

THE LIBRARY

Full Renaissance   *Sir Christopher Wren*

Stone   1676

Wren's Library, here seen from the 'Backs', belongs to his mature period, ranking among his civil and domestic buildings as equal to his work at Hampton Court and overshadowed only by Greenwich and Chelsea Hospitals. Like the other collegiate buildings at Cambridge that face the river, it closes the older courts of the College that are entered from the street, but the Trinity building is peculiar, as the pillared cloister of the lower storey occupies its entire width. The great doorways and iron-grilled openings of the river front give entry and light to the cloister; the Library, taking up the full length of the upper storey, being accessible from a staircase at the north end, approached from the other side of the building.

In this great design, Wren achieved monumental quality, not by the provision of an Order expressing the full height of the Library—an expedient that was ruled out by the lines of Nevile's Court—but by the more novel method of raising the treatment of the lower storey to the sill-height of the Library windows. The whole of the upper treatment differs from that on the Court side, being dominated by a continuous 'clearstorey' resting on a fine arrangement of horizontal lines enriched by the Doric entablatures —with their extremely effective triglyphs—of the three doorways connecting the building firmly to its base. Breadth is secured by the absence of any projections from the general wall surface except in these doorways, and by the provision of a cornice only —not a full entablature—at the wall-head; while the round-headed mullioned windows of the Library are brought to simplicity by framing them in rectangular recesses, with responses in the breaks of the crowning parapet.

There is a complete absence of sculptured ornament, but the delightful weathering is most effective; the pinks and yellows of the larger wall surfaces contrasting with the cool greys of the cornices and the grey-white of the stone parapet and the lead roof.

THE FRONT

Full Renaissance   1675–1697
(*Carolean to William and Mary*)
Brick and Stone

St Catharine's is the only College in Cambridge with a court that is open to a street: the range that usually closed-off a court was never completed. Cambridge has gained by this: the view of the large open space, enclosed on three sides by buildings which are given scale and depth by the gate piers of the front railings, is striking; especially when the late morning sun dispels their sombre effect and casts wide shadows across the west range, bringing its features into relief; the whole effect being increased by the set-back of the railings and gates from the street line.

Although it was completed slightly before that period, St Catharine's is more 'Queen Anne' in its feeling than anything else in Cambridge collegiate architecture—the brickwork, with stone sparingly introduced, the modillion cornices of the tiled roofs and the fine dormers, are completely in character. We must concede a Carolean form to the windows—each one divided into four, with mullion and transom—as it was not till the reign of Queen Anne that the use of the sash window became general.

The motive of a recessed range of buildings supported by two side wings coming out to the foreground, is the finest possible one for giving value to an emphasised central feature; and at St Catharine's the split-pediment★ over the archway of the front is handled largely, the most considerable piece of work in Cambridge that has 'Baroque' quality.

There are differences—both in the detailed character and in the dates—of the various elements of the Court as a whole, but the front was built at the beginning of the last quarter of the seventeenth century.

★ A pediment is 'split' when the side lines are designed not to meet at the centre: for 'broken pediments' see Pl. XXII.

85

ST CATHARINE'S COLLEGE XXII

FRONT TO QUEENS' LANE

Full Renaissance   *Late 17th Century*

Brick and Stone

The entrance to the College is now from Trumpington Street, but
the front here shown—the lengthened reverse of the one on the
previous plate—was originally the entrance one. The College has,
in fact, been turned round, because the east range on Trumpington
Street was never completed, and Queens' Lane became a bye-
street instead of a main thoroughfare.

Though it can only be seen properly in sharp perspective, this
Queens' Lane front is the finest Renaissance street façade in
Cambridge, and one that is peculiarly happy for a narrow street.
The central feature, built wholly of stone, has the right kind of
simplicity in its outer lines, relieved on the upper storey by
boldly-projecting Ionic pilasters, in place of the 'engaged'
Corinthian columns on the Court side. This admirable squareness
of treatment is enhanced by the pronounced vertical planes of the
cornice and pediment, but the central feature, though strong, is
not heavy, while, on the skyline, it dominates effectively the
powerful factor of the dormer windows which flank it on either
side; these, as usual in Early and Full Renaissance, avoiding
monotony by the rhythmical alternation of their treatment. Again
we have a 'baroque' touch in the broken pediments of the central
feature, but the main one is triangular and the smaller one of the
window below is segmental; in each case a reversal of the treatment in the side towards the Court.

The bold rusticated piers which flank the gateway, with their
ample cornices, serve as an efficient base to the whole; while the
general treatment of the façade supports the central feature
excellently, having sufficient relief—in plinth band, window
dressings, modillioned cornice and angle-quoins—to secure adequate balance.*

* See remarks under 'PLINTH' in Glossary.

87

Full Renaissance   1701–1702
    Oak

The most complete Chapel woodwork of the Full Renaissance in
Cambridge is at Christ's College; only excelled, in either University, by that at Trinity College, Oxford. Though it has been
fitted into a badly-lighted Mediaeval building, so that some feeling
of incongruity is unavoidable, and while some of the carving has
a certain crudity, a great deal of it is able to hold its own with
anything of the kind in England. The most disappointing element
in the woodwork of the Chapel as a whole is the treatment of the
east end—a weakness also found in some of the City churches of
London—but the wall treatment at the sides of the Sanctuary,
especially the relief carving below the entablature and its returns
on the east wall, are of the first quality; as is the organ-case on the
north wall.

The delicately-detailed panelling of the side walls of the Chapel
is returned at the west end, but the chief motive of this end—part
of which is shown in the sketch—is the entrance opening and its
two flanking features, the raised and emphasised seats for the
Master and President; this being an unvarying arrangement in
collegiate chapels, and one that gives a fine opportunity for an
important centralised effect at each end.

A design of this kind is not without its difficulties, but it has
been carried out here with conspicuous success.★ The pedestalled
Order treatments with their segmental pediments give great
dignity to the two seats, while the three main elements of the
design are linked together by the continuous entablature, the
skilful alignment of other moulded members, the oblong panels
above the seat niches, and the delightful relief carving in the
spandrels of the central arch; the carving in the moulded members
of the imposts being also of fine quality. It will be seen that the
carved arms of the seats have excellent responses in the ends of the
book-rests that terminate the scholars' seats.

★ A somewhat similar treatment to that shown here was used for the Roman
Arch at Timgad, in North Africa.

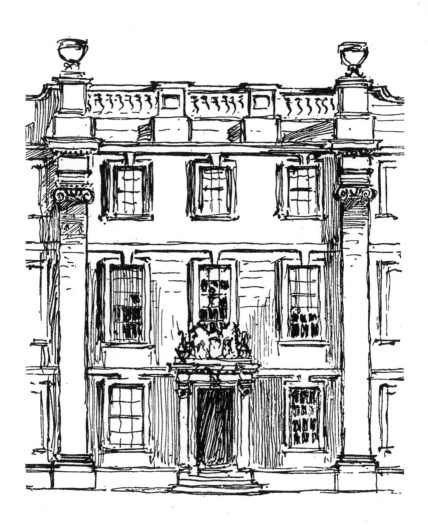

THE WESTMORELAND BUILDING

Early Georgian   1718–1722

    Stone

This south side of the Court of Emmanuel—the re-built 'Founder's Range'—shows Georgian architecture to advantage, by its sash windows in storeys of varying heights, stone window-surrounds, moulded sills, and keystones linked up to projecting wall-bands that give definition of storey-height; admirable proportion and simple but effective design being achieved by these comparatively simple means. The central feature shown here, raised a little higher than the rest of the range, is framed by the pilastered Ionic Order dominating the entire height and by the attic with its pedestals, balustrades and vases. Central interest is provided by the charming *bijou* of a doorway with its curved steps.

    The usual Georgian emphasis of the first floor (the *piano nobile*) and the accentuation of the windows of the two principal storeys by projecting breastworks below the window-sills are important elements in the design. The balance of horizontal and vertical elements is secure, and the enriched parts—the details of the great Order and its attic, and the heraldic set-piece over the doorway—give character to the whole composition.

    The whole feature is the most attractive thing of its kind in Cambridge. Pilasters of the scale employed are often blatant and tiresome; here, they are very quietly and yet tellingly decorative, friendly giants like the bearded men in 'the Broad' at Oxford. There are many buildings which are more or less of this kind in other English towns, and England would be much poorer without them, as they are the most important remaining visible reminders of the stateliness and orderliness of the early eighteenth century.

THE FELLOWS' BUILDING

Full Renaissance   *James Gibbs*, 1724
Stone

Great as was the Founder's conception for King's College, its completion, after the Chapel had been finished by his successors, was not realised till the eighteenth and nineteenth centuries; and then in a very different way. The amount of land that had been acquired by him, however, enabled this collegiate part of Cambridge to be the most spacious in the University, and with the distinction of having a river frontage as well as a street frontage. Starting from the south, Queens', King's, Clare, Trinity Hall, Trinity and St John's, form a noble continuous group from the 'Backs', of which King's is the grandest element. Seen from there, the great mass of the Chapel is on the left, and the early and late nineteenth century buildings, by Wilkins and Bodley★ respectively, are on the right; the link between the two elements being the Fellows' Building, part of a design that included one of similar character where the Wilkins Buildings now are.

It is remarkable that the schemes of Gibbs's rival and contemporary, Nicholas Hawksmoor—that were approved by Wren —were ignored, as the existing models and drawings by Hawksmoor, prepared about 1713, prove that he had gone into the matter thoroughly. Hawksmoor got his chance at Queen's College, Oxford; Gibbs at King's College and the Cambridge Senate House. The Fellows' Building—more commonly called in Cambridge 'Gibbs Building'—is an important example of his work; its overall length of 240 feet exceeding that of the Library at Trinity by over thirty feet, and having, most appropriately, no Order treatment except an accessory one that is used with telling effect in the central motive.

The treatment of the Court front of the building is exactly similar, but the wider spacing of the windows on the river front secures greater breadth to a design that is admirable in its proportion and its serenity, as well as in the handling of its details.

★ Recently extended by Mr Kennedy.

Full Renaissance

Stone

James Gibbs

1719—1730

There are few ecclesiastical buildings and still fewer civil buildings of Renaissance or Modern times that are based directly on the idea of the Classical temple. The Senate House at Cambridge belongs to that type, which, alternatively, could be called the rectangular box type with a single Order treatment, and of such —among civil examples—the seventeenth century 'Hall of the Knights' at Stockholm is perhaps the most distinguished. In this type of building, we find a uniform Order that embraces the whole height, and a simple, low-pitched roof with a pediment at each end. These are the essentials and they form a motive of such strength that the remainder of the treatment is reduced to comparatively narrow limits.

In the Cambridge Senate House, it was a practical requirement that there should be a ceremonial entrance in the centre of the long front (the side of the 'temple') in addition to the ordinary entrance at the street front, and Gibbs took full advantage of this by making a repeat of his end treatment at the ceremonial entrance. The pedimented break, with four engaged fluted columns, relieves the monotony of the long wall and also gives meaning to the purposes of the building, while the windows, in two tiers, express practically the interior arrangement with its gallery; and it will be seen that the round-headed windows in the upper tier have the archivolt mouldings continuous with those of the jambs, as in Wren's Chapel at Pembroke College (Pl. XVII). The details and accessories were carried out with Gibbs's usual care and refinement, the carving and urns of the pediments being in unexceptionable taste.

The building stands in fine relation to the old University Library—now the Old Schools—while the proximity of the contrasting turrets of King's College Chapel secures, from the south, the most matchless street view that Cambridge possesses.

PART OF THE EAST FRONT

Late Renaissance   *Stephen Wright*

Stone   1754–1758

An account of the rival schemes for the completion of the east
side of the mediaeval building known as the Schools Quadrangle,
which, until 1935, was the University Library, can be found else-
where;* for the present purpose, attention need be called only to
the projecting part that forms the centre of the front, providing
a covered walk on the ground floor and a part of what, until 1935,
was known as the 'East Room' of the Library. This ingenuity in
planning secured not only increased accommodation, but gave an
opportunity for architectural treatment; and in the result, a comparatively unknown architect produced a building that, for its
size, can hold its own with anything in England.

One notices the admirable balance of the whole composition
and a liveliness, as of arrested motion, that can only be secured
by the judicious use of arched forms. These qualities, being
enhanced by the detailed treatment—the strengthening of the projecting part of the ground storey by rusticated stonework, and the
upper storey with its fine windows and with its strong emphasis
at top and bottom—give distinction to a building that would be
noticeable anywhere, and is particularly so in its actual setting.
Perhaps its most outstanding quality is the 'festal look'† given
to the top treatment, where the balustraded parapet and its urns
get their fullest value from the splendid festooned carving below
the cornice, suspended as a deep frieze unhampered by an architrave.

The Portland stone has weathered beautifully, so that the front
is expressive in its texture as well as in its form; in addition, the
dark weather-drips are particularly effective.

* Willis and Clark, Vol. III, pp. 62–6.
† A happy expression, once used in a different connection, by the late
Prof. Baldwin Brown.

Late Renaissance with   *James Essex, 1766–1770*

     Tudor elements   *(Oriel, c. 1509)*

        Stone

A description of Cambridge architecture that omitted any reference to James Essex would be incomplete. Though hardly known outside Cambridge, Essex left a permanent mark on five Colleges—Trinity Hall, Trinity, Christ's, Emmanuel and Peterhouse—and he made an important contribution to Cambridge architecture in the west range of Emmanuel College, that has a stone front of nearly 180 feet on St Andrew's Street. Possibly for lack of incentive or of money, he was not so successful in his building at Queens' or in the Guildhall, but he was handicapped by having to use a poor quality of light brick in both of these.

Essex's work was never distinguished, but his stone treatments were always pleasant; and it is fortunate that he practised in the later half of the eighteenth century, when the orderliness of Georgian building was thoroughly understood. For the most part he simply re-faced the fronts of earlier buildings in the manner of his time, but at Christ's, the corbelling, carved breastwork and cornice of the oriel window in the Master's Lodge—dating from the time of the Foundress—were not only saved, but were skilfully incorporated by Essex with the reconstructed bay window and parapet of his building; which restraint had its reward, as the whole feature, including the doorway below it, gives emphasis just where it is required, and balances the higher part of the north range with its important entrance to the ante-chapel.*

The parapet of the Master's Lodge is a simplified version of the original battlemented one, and is in character with the tiled roof and its dormers. The chimney-stack at the gable-end of the Lodge and the uniform alignment of the ground floor windows are valuable for linking the two ranges together.

* Essex was no barbarian, as can be seen in his remodelling of the end of the Founder's range at Emmanuel College; he retained most of the original elements and made this end the finish of his street front, on the south, making the north end of his building to correspond with it.

CORPUS CHRISTI COLLEGE XXIX

THE FRONT

Gothic Revival

Stone

William Wilkins

1823–1827

Though this plate does not pretend to give an adequate impression of the view looking up King's Parade—which, like all lovely street views, is particularly susceptible to the effects of sunlight and shadow—it shows how the cliff-like mass of Corpus Christi College dominates the east side of the street; framing, on that side, the magic picture disclosed by the street bend, while its turrets balance the emphatic verticality of King's College Chapel.

The Gothic Revival in England ran parallel to the Classic Revival, and similarly attempted adaptability for all kinds of buildings. The latest phase of this Revival, as applied to civil and domestic buildings, can be seen at Cambridge in the works of Alfred Waterhouse at Caius, Pembroke and Girton Colleges, and of Bodley at King's College. William Wilkins, a most able exponent of the Classic Revival, and the architect of Downing College, Cambridge, is unique for his renouncing of Classicism for collegiate purposes and becoming in his last years a convinced exponent of the Gothic school; moreover, Cambridge is unique in possessing all his efforts in this direction. By his work on the fronts of King's and Corpus Christi Colleges, Wilkins made notable contributions to the street architecture of Cambridge.

The largeness of handling that can be seen in all Wilkins's work is conspicuous in the Corpus front.* The strong horizontal lines of the base-courses are particularly valuable in binding together the three main vertical elements of a composition acting as an admirable foil to the more varied elements on the other side of the street; culminating in Wilkins's screen and gateway and the turrets of King's, the chestnut tree, the Senate House, and the tower of St John's College Chapel.

* The attic storey, designed with success by Mr T. H. Lyon, was added in the present century.

Classic Revival   *George Basevi*

Stone   1837–1843*

Cambridge is fortunate in possessing the Fitzwilliam Museum, certainly one of the most complete and carefully-studied compositions of its period. Externally, it is best known by the majestic scale of its portico on Trumpington Street, but—if full justice is to be done to it—it must be regarded as a foursquare structure. It is true that the front, with its great flight of steps and the pedestalled lions which form its lateral terminations, is the most conspicuous feature, but the recurrence of the pilastered Order treatment at the western corners, and the continuous entablature and attic, give immense value to the building as a whole, a value increased by the uprising square mass of the upper part of the internal staircase. Here, as at St George's Hall, Liverpool,† the classic portico and pediment have their grand and original Greek function of appearing to terminate the full horizontal length of the building; also—again as at St George's Hall, to which, in its main lines, the Fitzwilliam has a certain resemblance—we find that rare feature, a fully-sculptured pediment.

The large expanse of wall surface at the side, unwindowed in the upper storey, called for careful treatment. The strong horizontal element demanded by the Classical formula is, of course, insistent, but the gentle vertical emphasis of the delicately-detailed niches is particularly happy. Below the enriched wall-band, on which the niches stand, is a range of triple windows, fully pilastered and pedimented. The whole building owes not a little to the carefully-designed frontage line, with its massive gate piers, balustrading and fine cast-iron work, that give scale and dignity to the main mass.

* The whole of the exterior is substantially Basevi's, though after his death in 1845, C. R. Cockerell (in 1847) and E. M. Barry (in 1871) certainly carried out work inside the building.
† Designed by Harvey Lonsdale Elmes in 1839.

THE MEMORIAL COURT

Modern (20th Century)   *Sir Giles Scott*
Brick and Stone   1928–1932

The Memorial Court of Clare College, which has its front to Queens' Road, facing the 'Backs', has been selected as a type of Modern architecture; firstly, because—even apart from its association with another building by the same designer*—it is the most important collegiate work by a single architect in Cambridge; secondly, because, being so considerable in extent, it is almost like a complete College; and lastly, because, being so detached from the older Colleges, there was no question of the necessity or advisability of treating it in a markedly traditional or stylistic way. When dealing with Cambridge, the appropriateness of selecting a collegiate building is obvious.

For various reasons, a particularly open type of lay-out was adopted, and the view, taken from the driveway leading to the University Library, shows mainly the two contracted wings of the College buildings that complete them towards the west; forming symmetrical units that are connected by monumentally-treated gates, facing the Library and in axial relation with it and with the memorial archway of the front to Queens' Road. On the right, a portion of the lower building forming the south range of the wider portion of the court can be seen.

The buildings are delightful in texture and colour, and they have been most carefully designed; but their manner is one that does not convey any pronounced idea of a particular period or style, though there is a happy suggestion of the older Clare in the fine roofs and chimney-stacks. Here we can see a Modern building that might be called 'functional', in the fullest sense of the term; which, if it must be used, should have a much wider application than that of the catchword now in use.

* The University Library.

GLOSSARY*

ABACUS (Pl. ABACI): the top member of the capital of a column, pilaster or shaft, forming a flat pad to give a good bearing to the structure of the arch or lintel above.

ARCHITRAVE: primarily, the lowest or 'beam' element in a Classical or Renaissance 'Entablature' (*q.v.*); also a similar but smaller treatment on the head and sides of a Classical or Renaissance window or door, whether or not it has a frieze and cornice in addition (see Fig. 10, and the windows in Pl. XVIII). In modern architectural practice, the term applies to any trimming round a rectangular opening.

ARCHIVOLT: the treatment of a Renaissance arch that corresponds with that of a lintel in the same manner (architrave, *q.v.*, and Fig. 11).

ATTIC: in Classical or Renaissance architecture, the cresting, or uppermost wall treatment, that is above the highest cornice or entablature; thus, an attic may be anything from a balustrade or parapet to a low wall containing panelling, ornament, or small windows lighting a storey that is usually (in such a case) partly in the roof.

BALL-FLOWER: in Decorated Gothic, an enrichment worked in a hollow moulding and recurring at intervals, consisting of a spherical form with a lipped trefoil sinking cut on the front; probably a conventional rendering of a partly-opened bud.

BARNWELL PRIORY: a twelfth century re-foundation, of which a few remains still exist near the junction of Newmarket Road with Abbey Road. It existed till the Dissolution; Richard the Second held a Parliament there in 1388.

BAROQUE: Renaissance art and architecture that originated in Rome in the third quarter of the sixteenth century, and spread to Austria, Germany and France during the seventeenth and early eighteenth centuries. It aimed at centrality of emphasis and a

* All the definitions are my own, but I have profited by consulting Mr T. D. Atkinson's *Glossary of English Architecture* (Methuen, 1906). T. F.

rhythmical association of subsidiary elements; it can be seen to best advantage, architecturally, in set-pieces such as façades and monuments.

BEAD AND REEL: in Classical or Renaissance architecture, an enrichment on a small bead moulding (see Fig. 11).

BRUNELLESCHI, FILIPPO: the first great architect of the Renaissance, who designed churches in Florence in the purest manner of the Style as early as 1425; most famous for the dome which he designed in 1420, and afterwards constructed, for Florence Cathedral.

CLUNCH: a soft white limestone indigenous to the Cambridge district, much used for internal work in the Middle Ages; used also for external work in rough walls, but occasionally for architectural detail. It weathers badly, but its large proportion of pure lime makes it almost indestructible.

CONSOLE: a Classical or Renaissance form of ornamental bracket, used vertically, under the ends of the cornice of a door or window. The term is used for Pl. XIX, because the form is similar, though reversed.

CORBEL: a stone (usually shaped or carved) or a brick, built into a wall but standing out from it, to carry a projection from the wall surface above the corbel, or to carry another corbel or series of corbels for the same purpose. The terms 'corbelling' or 'corbelled' are used when corbels are built in continuous lines. Thus, an oriel (*q.v.*) is corbelled out from a wall.

CORBEL TABLE: in Gothic architecture, recurrent corbels (*q.v.*) carrying a continuous projecting stone-course (the 'table'), that acted as a drip or supported a stone parapet.

CROCKET: a spur: in Early English Gothic, a comparatively simple sprouting form; in Decorated and Perpendicular Gothic, a larger, more complicated and more richly-carved form, that (especially in Decorated) was used profusely for interior as well as exterior work, on hood-moulds, etc. See Pl. XI for a Perpendicular treatment.

CUSP: in Gothic architecture, the point formed by the meeting of two adjacent 'foils' or 'foliations' proceeding from a primary form that may be straight or curved; a circular primary form producing a cusped 'trefoil', 'quatrefoil', etc. Simple cusping of window tracery is shown in Figs. 4 and 5; and of stone relief-carving in Fig. 6. In late Decorated work, features of special emphasis—such as sedilia in chancels—sometimes had double cusping, i.e. the first foliations were also foliated. In the geometrical tracery of Early English Gothic, cusping had nobility of form; in some of the later work described above, though great richness was produced, there was a tendency to over-elaboration (see p. 29).

DENTILS: in Classical or Renaissance architecture, closely-recurrent small rectangular brackets, forming an enrichment in cornices (see Fig. 11).

DOG-TOOTH: a small square pyramidal enrichment in Early English Gothic, worked in a hollow moulding, the square being cut to form four pointed 'leaves' or 'teeth'. As the squares were worked close together, the whole produced a continuous and not, like the ball-flower (q.v.), a widely recurrent enrichment.

EGG AND TONGUE: in Classical or Renaissance architecture, a carved enrichment used on a convex moulding (ovolo), consisting of recurrent egg-shaped forms with 'tongues' or 'darts' between them.

ENGAGED COLUMN: a column in an Order (q.v.) treatment which is partly attached to the wall.

ENTABLATURE: the horizontal or beam element in Classical or Renaissance Order treatments, composed, when complete, of architrave (lowest member and actual 'beam'), frieze (intermediate member) and cornice (crowning member). Sometimes the frieze was omitted. The Fitzwilliam Museum (Pl. XXX) shows a Classical building carrying a full entablature, both with and without Orders (see p. 22).

ETRUSCAN WORK: the architecture of Etruria, in Central Italy, which influenced that of Rome in many ways.

FINIAL: an ornamental termination.

GABLE: the walled end of a 'pitched' (i.e. considerably sloped) roof; therefore, triangular in general form. If carried above the roof, it may either be parallel with the roof slopes, or, as in

'Dutch' gables, be shaped in various ways. If not carried above the roof, the slates or tiles of the roof-covering project slightly beyond the wall-face, or 'gable-end', forming a 'verge'.

HADRIAN: Emperor of Rome, A.D. 117 to 138. He succeeded Trajan, and, under these two, Roman architecture made vast strides in constructive methods; also reaching its culminating point in purity of style.

IMPOST: in its simplest expression, a projecting pad-stone at the top of the jamb (*q.v.*) of an arched opening, from where one side of the arch springs. Imposts can be moulded or unmoulded (see Fig. 11 and Pl. XXVII).

INBAND AND OUTBAND: see 'QUOINS'.

JAMB: the side of an opening (door or window), including both its front and its return or reveal (*q.v.*)—see Fig. 11. Thus a jamb would include both an architrave (*q.v.*) and a reveal in a Renaissance opening; or any mouldings (as in Mediaeval architecture) that might take the place of an architrave, and would be termed 'jamb mouldings'.

LEAF AND TONGUE: in Classical or Renaissance architecture, a carved enrichment used on a curve of contrary flexure (*cyma reversa*), consisting of recurrent leaf-like forms with 'tongues' or 'darts' between them.

LIERNE RIBS: ribs, sometimes non-constructional, introduced in fourteenth century Gothic and crossing vault-spandrels (vault, *q.v.*), thus producing a richer pattern.

LONG AND SHORT WORK: in Saxon architecture, corner stones or jamb stones (*q.v.*) placed lengthways horizontally and vertically, in alternate courses (see Pl. I).

MODILLION: in Classical or Renaissance architecture, (*a*) a bracket, designed like a console (*q.v.*) and used horizontally and recurrently under the top member of a cornice; (*b*) a bracket serving a similar function, but of plain rectangular form.

MOULDINGS (MOULDED): see p. 11.

MULLION: vertical structural member in a window (see Fig. 10).

ORDER: see 'ENTABLATURE', and p. 22.

ORIEL: a projecting window that is corbelled out from a wall (corbel, *q.v.*).

PANES: (*a*) divisions of window glazing; (*b*) compartments of a cloister (see Pl. X).

PIER: a main support or independent mass that is larger than a column, or a tall projection from a wall that is not a pilaster (*q.v.*). See Descriptions to Plates XVIII, XIX and XXII for different applications of the term.

PIER ARCHES: in Gothic architecture, the series of arches dividing the nave from the aisles of a cathedral or large monastic church. In parish churches, the term 'nave arcading' is usually employed, and is equally good for all purposes.

PILASTER (see also STRIP-PILASTER): in Classical or Renaissance architecture, a flat squared projection having a design similar or sympathetic with that of the column of an Order (*q.v.*). Thus, pilasters can be used for Order treatments instead of columns.

PLINTH (PLINTH BAND): the base of a building or pier, usually projecting and sometimes finished with a moulded capping or 'plinth course', or having other moulded members. The term 'plinth band' used for the Queens' Lane front of St Catharine's (p. 87) is not strictly correct, as this band really forms the division of a high 'base' or ground storey, and a 'main wall-field' or upper floors (see p. 22); the actual plinth being about three feet high and not visible through the iron railings in the drawing. A plain plinth is shown in Pl. XXVII.

PURBECK MARBLE: a dense grey or brownish-grey limestone from the Isle of Purbeck in Dorsetshire, much used in Early English and occasionally (as at Ely Cathedral) in later Gothic. It takes a polish, but in Salisbury and Lincoln Cathedrals its effect, in contrast with whiter stone, was ruined in the nineteenth century by blackening it with oil.

QUOINS: corner stones, which are either plain and flush with the wall, or project slightly as rustication (*q.v.*). In brick buildings, quoins can be formed of three or more courses of bricks, slightly projecting. Quoins are arranged as 'inband' and 'outband'; inband being the stones or brick courses that are narrow on the face but wide on the return (*q.v.*) or reveal (*q.v.*), and outband those that show a reverse treatment (see Pl. XI).

RELIEVING ARCH: an arch over a door or window opening that is built into the walling above it to 'relieve' the head of the opening from direct weight (see Pl. XVI, as those in Pl. X and Fig. 5 are really 'outer arches').

RETURN: any abrupt break in a building, or feature of a building. Thus (*a*) the front of a building is 'returned' at a corner; or (*b*) a continuous horizontal moulding has a 'returned' projection when worked round a pilaster.

REVEAL: the depth, internal or external, from wall-face to frame or filling, on the side of a door or window opening.

RUSTICATION: literally, and permissibly, a rough face-tooling of squared masonry to give an effect of strength; or, for a similar purpose, and in its commoner application, slightly projecting courses of 'ashlar' (i.e. regular and finely-finished) masonry, with either a squared or V sinking at the bed-joints and (usually) vertical joints, thus defining each course or stone. Sometimes this last treatment is given a slightly roughened face.

SAMARRA: an early Moslem palace of great extent and magnificence, on the river Tigris in northern Mesopotamia.

SAN GALLI: Antonio da San Gallo (the Elder); his brother, Giuliano da San Gallo; and his nephew, Antonio da San Gallo (the Younger): all famous architects of the earlier and later middle period of the Italian Renaissance, practising in the last quarter of the fifteenth century and the first half of the sixteenth.

SILL-TABLE: a flat window-sill of stone filling up the whole depth of the internal reveal (*q.v.*) of a window.

SOLIDS AND VOIDS: the built-up and open (door and window) elements on the face of a building, in their respective gross total areas.

SPALATO: a town (now called Split) in Dalmatia, on the eastern side of the Adriatic Sea. The reference here is to its famous building—the Palace of Diocletian, erected c. A.D. 300—on which the English architect Robert Adam published a large illustrated folio, in 1764.

SPANDREL: (a) the space, roughly triangular, between one half of an arch and a squared definition enclosing it; the latter, in Perpendicular Gothic architecture, may be formed by a label (see Fig. 6), and in Renaissance architecture, by a column or pilaster and entablature (see Pl. XXIII); (b) any approximately triangular space such as a filling in a vault (q.v.).

STRING-COURSE: a continuous projecting course, usually moulded, in a stone or brick wall.

STRIP-PILASTER: a very narrow projection from a wall, found in Saxon architecture. In Pl. I it acts in place of an 'engaged column' (q.v.) by giving emphasis to each side of the Arch, but such 'pilasters' had their origin in the distrust of building long stretches of walling without breaks.

TEMPERA: a form of water paint, mixed with white of egg, and applied to a fine plaster surface or on wood, much used in the Middle Ages.

TRACERY: stone patterning in Gothic windows; see pp. 9, 10.

TRANSOM: see p. 11 n.

TRIFORIUM: in Mediaeval architecture, the intermediate arcaded corridor or gallery between the pier arches (q.v.) and the 'clear-storey' (high range of windows above the aisles); most conspicuous in the Norman and Early English periods, but usually found only in very large churches or cathedrals; rarely met with after the thirteenth century, and, in its latest development, a blocked arcade of minor character.

TRIGLYPHS: the vertical members in the frieze of a Doric entablature (q.v.), alternating regularly with the 'metopes' or square interspaces; so-called because each one has two 'glyphs' or channellings, and two half-glyphs, in front.

VAULT: an arched ceiling, usually of stone or brick; if continuous and semicircular in cross section, a 'barrel' vault, an early form rare in English architecture; vaulting being usually set-out in 'bays' or compartments, each bay consisting of two intersecting barrel vaults, one at right angles to the other, which produced 'groins' or salient angles at the intersections. In Norman Romanesque, the round arches necessitated square vault bays: in

Gothic, the greater height proportion and adaptability of pointed arches secured safer building in vault bays, which could be either square or rectangular.

Groins were carefully built with worked stone, and except in some Norman cellar vaults, formed projecting moulded 'diagonal ribs'—the kernel of the whole construction—the spaces between the ribs being 'vault-filling' or 'vault-spandrels'. The pointed rib-vault is the most important fact in the Gothic style, but the naves of only outstanding churches or cathedrals were stone-vaulted, though aisle vaulting was more usual, even in Norman churches, in which nave vaulting was rarely attempted. 'Cross ribs' were introduced at the end of the twelfth century; 'ridge ribs' and 'intermediate ribs' (the latter springing from the same points as the main or diagonal ribs), at the end of the thirteenth century.

VAULTING SHAFT: in Gothic architecture, a large shaft (see p. 12), attached to an internal wall, that carried the springing of the ribs of a vault compartment; it was usually taken down to the floor, but sometimes corbelled (q.v.) at a higher level.

WINDOW DRESSINGS: a general term for the 'dressed' or finished stonework, including the head, jambs (q.v.) and sill.

INDEX

Names in small capitals are also in the Glossary
Personal names are in italics

Near East(ern), 20, 21, 25, 45
Norman architecture, 5, 6, 7, 8 n., 9, 11, 12, 25, 35, 41 N. 6, 47, 49
Northwold, Bishop Hugh of, 26
Norwich Cathedral, 27

Orders, 22, 23, 40 N. 3, 83, 91, 93, 95, 103
Oriental sources, 21
Ottoman Turks, 21
OXFORD, 3, 69, 73
  'Broad', the, 91
  Cathedral (Christ Church), 41 N. 6
  Queen's College, 29, 93
  St John's College, 61
  Trinity College, 89

Paint, use of, 34, 35
Palladio, Andrea, 40 N. 3
Parker, J. H., 8 n.
Perpendicular Gothic, 8 and n., 10, 11, 12, 28, 57, 59, 63, 65
Plasterwork, 33–35
Prior, E. S. and *Gardner, A.*, 25 n.
Pugin, A. W., 51

'Quattro Cento', 30
Queen Anne period, 17, 85

Renaissance architecture, 4, 13, 16, 17, 18, 20, 23 and n., 24, 28, 29, 33, 36, 41 n. 8, 61, 71, 73, 75, 77, 79, 81, 83, 85, 87, 89, 93, 95, 97, 99
Restoration, the, 18
Revival, 36
Rickman, T. S., 41 N. 9
Roman architecture (and Rome), 4, 5, 20, 21, 32, 45
Romanesque architecture, 4, 5, 7, 25, 45, 47, 49

St George's Chapel, Windsor, 59
St Luke's Church, Chelsea, 38

CAMBRIDGE: PRINTED BY W. LEWIS, M.A., AT THE UNIVERSITY PRESS

For EU product safety concerns, contact us at Calle de José Abascal, 56–1°, 28003 Madrid, Spain or eugpsr@cambridge.org.

www.ingramcontent.com/pod-product-compliance
Ingram Content Group UK Ltd.
Pitfield, Milton Keynes, MK11 3LW, UK
UKHW012338130625
459647UK00009B/380